'Stamp has described how Lu[...]
to the Missing of the Somm[...]
and as "saturated in melancholy" as the monument[...]
Far more than a work of pure architectural history, this
beautifully poignant book illuminates the tragedy of the
Great War, and tells us much about its aftermath. It is a
truly classical piece of prose, a tragic chorus on the Somme
which reverberates on the battlefields of today' A. N. Wilson

'A brilliant achievement ... I felt instantly at one with [the]
approach and treatment. It was such a clever idea ... to treat
Lutyens through Thiepval.' John Keegan

'An invaluable, detailed and illuminating study of how the
memorial came to be built and how its effects are achieved'
Geoff Dyer, *Guardian*

'Stamp's book is devoted to a single one of the thousands
of memorials that now dot the battlefield, Lutyens's
stupendous arch at Thiepval that records the names of
over 73,000 British and South African soldiers who were
killed on the Somme but have no known graves. As a piece
of architectural analysis, it is impressive' M. R. D. Foot,
Spectator

'A passionate and unusual book ... [an] eloquent account of
the genius of the vision of Lutyens ... who created in the
Monument to the Missing at Thiepval the central metaphor
of a generation's experience of appalling loss' Tim Gardham,
Observer

'Moving and eloquent' Nigel Jones, *Literary Review*

GAVIN STAMP is an architectural historian and writer, and
was made an honorary professor by both the Universities of
Glasgow and Cambridge. His books include *Edwin Lutyens'
Country Houses*, *Gothic for the Steam Age*, *Alexander 'Greek'
Thomson*, *An Architect of Promise*, *The Changing Metropolis*,
Anti-Ugly and *Telephone Boxes*.

WONDERS OF THE WORLD

....

THE MEMORIAL TO THE MISSING OF THE SOMME

GAVIN STAMP

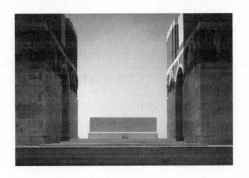

P

PROFILE BOOKS

This revised paperback edition published in 2016

First published in Great Britain in 2006 by
Profile Books Ltd
3 Holford Yard
Bevin Way
London WC1X 9HD
www.profilebooks.com

1 3 5 7 9 10 8 6 4 2

Typeset in Caslon by MacGuru Ltd
info@macguru.org.uk
Designed by Peter Campbell
Printed and bound in Great Britain by
CPI Group (UK) Ltd, Croydon CR0 4YY

A CIP catalogue record for this book is available from the
British Library.

ISBN 978 1 78125 506 3
eISBN 978 1 84765 060 3

CONTENTS

PREFACE

The Memorial to the Missing of the Somme was first published in 2006 in Profile's 'Wonders of the World' series. This second, revised edition is published a decade later to coincide with the centenary of the Battle of the Somme. The original text has been corrected and updated but is largely unchanged. An Afterword has, however, been added which explores the continuing significance of the extraordinary monument the British raised at Thiepval on the Somme – social, historical and architectural – in the context of the hundredth anniversary of the catastrophic struggle whose resonances never seem to fade: the Great War of 1914–1918.

The areas fought over during the Battle of the Somme

INTRODUCTION

The village of Thiepval lies some four miles north of the town of Albert in the *département* of Somme, part of what was once the province of Picardy in northern France. It stands 490 feet above sea level on a ridge on the chalk plateau which rises above the east bank of the valley of the river Ancre, a tributary of the languid Somme, which it joins at Corbie to the south-west. A century ago, there was a small, semi-feudal farming community here with a population of about two hundred living in some sixty houses, and the village could boast, as well as its modern church, a large seventeenth-century *château*, the home of the Comte de Bréda. Summer visitors, who came to fish or swim in the Ancre or to walk or ride in the quiet rolling, rural downland, came to Thiepval principally for its renowned *pâtisserie*.

Today, some seventy people live in the commune of Thiepval, but there is no trace of the *château* or of any building older than the 1930s: everything above ground was wiped out during the Great War of 1914–18. There is now a new church, a small brick building with a rugged war memorial built into the south-west corner of its saddle-back tower. Completed in 1933, it is appropriately dedicated to Our Lady of Peace. But the principal landmark in the village – indeed, the structure which dominates the surrounding countryside

1. The Thiepval Arch as newly completed.

– is not a church steeple but an extraordinary pile of red brick and white stone. From some angles, it looks like a tall tower rising above the trees; from others it looks like a massive stepped ziggurat; but seen from the east or from the railway which runs along the valley from Arras to Albert – once part of a main line from Brussels to Paris before the advent of the TGV – it is revealed on its principal axis as a tall, thin arch rising into the sky, poised high above flanking blocks of masonry.

From closer to, it is seen that the structure consists not of one arch but is penetrated on all sides by a series of arched tunnels, all of different sizes. Above the giant arch rises a tower, on the top of which are two poles, flying the *tricolore* and the Union flag. Just below, framed between piers of brick flanked by stone wreaths, is a large stone tablet which bears the inscription, cut in fine Roman capitals, 'AUX ARMEES FRANÇAISE ET BRITANNIQUE L'EMPIRE BRITANNIQUE RECONNAISSANT'. Below this is a band of stone, bearing the dates 1914 and 1918 each side of a carved crown. And, further down, running along a stone string course at the level of the springing of the largest of the arched tunnels which penetrate the mass in two directions, more Roman capital letters explain that this most complicated and awesome structure is dedicated to 'THE MISSING OF THE SOMME'.

For what stands at Thiepval is a war memorial – perhaps the ultimate British war memorial. It commemorates a terrible event which changed the course of British history. Carved on the stone panels which line the inner faces of the sixteen massive piers formed by the interconnecting tunnels are the names of over 73,000 British soldiers most of whom disappeared in the desperate struggles which took place around here a century ago in 1916 – men whose bodies could not be found or identified. They were but some of the huge casualties (420,000 British dead and wounded) in an unresolved exercise in industrialised slaughter which we have learned to call the Battle of the Somme – victims of one extended campaign in the four-year-long struggle between Christian nations of Europe waged with unprecedented ruthlessness by their governments.

When viewed on one of the principal axes, the Thiepval Memorial can be appreciated as a composition of open arches, yet when seen from an angle, up close, it seems intimidatingly solid, with cubic masses of masonry building up on alternate axes to create a vast, pyramid-like structure of brick and stone. Nothing could be more massive and powerful, rooted to the ground. Yet at the very centre of the monument, where the largest tunnels converge and where wreaths of artificial red poppies always seem to lie on the steps that lead up to a great stone altar which bears the inscription 'THEIR NAME LIVETH FOR EVERMORE', mass is somehow dissolved. The visitor stands beneath a high stone vault resting on solid brick walls but is mostly conscious of space and sky as he, or she, looks out through the arches in each direction – north, south, east, west – over the placid, rural landscape which was once pulverised by weeks and weeks of shell-fire and soaked in the blood of tens of thousands of young men – British, French, German – who died in and around this spot in horrible and inexcusable circumstances. Thiepval surely ought to be haunted; as it is, the place is saturated in melancholy, and the monument reverberates with a sense of tragedy.

Below the high stone vaults, the brick walls carry large carved stone wreaths containing names of the nearby villages

2. The pyramidal, ziggurat profile of the Memorial seen on the diagonal through newly planted trees in the 1930s.

and woods where bloody battles took place in 1916: Beaumont-Hamel, Morval, Courcelette, Pozières, Flers, Delville Wood, Mametz, and so on. But these walls are also penetrated by the smaller arches, or tunnels, so that the visitor eventually appreciates that the compact, rectangular plan of the monument is formed by a grid of two intersecting sets of three tunnels – of different sizes – which separate sixteen solid piers of masonry. And, below the brickwork, every wall of these piers is faced in Portland stone, imported from England, into which are carved names: thousands and thousands of names, like wallpaper, listing some of those British soldiers who were not just casualties in this area between 1915 and 1918 but who simply disappeared, who have no known grave, whose bodies could not be found or identified: 73,357 names.

Almost all these names are of volunteers. Many of the men who went over the top on 1 July 1916 – the First Day of the Battle of the Somme – belonged to those battalions of 'Pals' or 'Chums': men who enlisted together from all over Britain and who had been promised that 'those who joined together would serve together'. They had all responded to the call for volunteers made by Lord Kitchener, Secretary of State for War, in August 1914 to augment Britain's small professional army already fighting in France and Belgium. It was this 'New Army' of civilians – idealistic and enthusiastic – that first went into battle on the Somme, and was decimated. The Thiepval memorial therefore also commemorates a loss of innocence. The date 1 July 1916 is one of the defining, polemical moments in British history, when that volunteer army, educated and skilled, containing many of the brightest and best in their country, was tested – and wasted. Everything was changed by the failure and slaughter of that day. As the historian John Keegan has written, 'To the British, it was and would remain their greatest military tragedy of the twentieth century, indeed of their national military history. […] The Somme marked the end of an age of vital optimism in British life that has never been recovered.'

The Memorial to the Missing of the Somme rises to a height of 140 feet above its basement terrace. It is therefore, and quite deliberately, fractionally smaller than the Arc de Triomphe, the colossal arch, 152 feet tall, in the Champs Elysées in Paris commissioned by the Emperor Napoleon and begun in 1806 to celebrate his victories over the rest of Europe. Consecrated to the glory of the French armies and designed by J.-F.-T. Chalgrin on the model of a Roman triumphal arch, the Arc de Triomphe is an essentially crude conception, if elegant in detail. It is but a giant slab of masonry, cut through by a large arched tunnel, with a smaller lateral tunnel running cross-ways; the composition is solid, static. The Memorial to the Missing of the Somme, in contrast, is a dynamic structure and one without precise historical precedent; its form is created by a carefully composed building up of cubic masses, governed by a most subtle aesthetic sensibility and by complex geometry, while the carefully arranged hierarchy of arches aligned on two axes seems properly structural, fulfilling a purpose and carrying weight.

More to the point, perhaps, is that there is no triumph about the arch at Thiepval because there was no triumph, no real victory, on the Somme in 1916. After five months, some six or seven miles of pulverised muddy territory had been gained, at a cost of 420,000 British and 204,000 French casualties. The German front line had been driven back, but remained almost as impregnable as before. The breakthrough,

3. The Arc de Triomphe de l'Etoile in Paris: a colossal slab of masonry with arches cut through it begun by Napoleon to glorify his military conquests.

so confidently expected by the British commander-in-chief, Sir Douglas Haig, remained as elusive as ever. At the Place de l'Etoile, the inside faces of the arch are carved with the names of Napoleon's generals and of the sites of ninety-six victories. At Thiepval, however, the names carved inside those giant wreaths are of nearby places where desperate struggles occurred, which saw acts of heroism and of vicious brutality, where men were machine-gunned, gassed, bombed, bayoneted, shot, or blown to pieces by grenades or high explosive, or cut up by shrapnel, or fell, burning, out of the sky – so often to little real purpose. And the names carved below are not those of generals and high-ranking officers, nor, indeed, those necessarily of heroes – to use that word now so debased by being indiscriminately applied to anyone serving in a British uniform – but of ordinary soldiers, mostly volunteers, some conscripts, who were caught up and did their duty in a cataclysmic struggle between nations.

On one level, therefore, the Thiepval arch is a positive monument, for it commemorates individuals. Like all the war cemeteries and other Memorials to the Missing created by the Imperial War Graves Commission after the war finally ended in November 1918, by bearing names carved in stone it asserts the significance of each life, however callously and incompetently that life may have been squandered by those in authority. Although its language of expression was rooted in the past, in the Classical tradition developed and handed down by the Romans almost two millennia earlier, this memorial could only have been created in the twentieth century, a century which may well have been one of unprecedented slaughter and inhumanity but which was also marked – at least in what we call the West – by a certain respect for individual human lives. The Memorial to the Missing of the Somme is an architectural statement which is at once timeless and modern, at once terrible and optimistic, totalitarian and democratic, brutal and civilised. An artistic creation of a very high order, it is one of the supreme architectural expressions of the European tragedy of the Great War of 1914–18.

Built between 1929 and 1932, the arch at Thiepval was designed by Edwin Lutyens, surely the greatest British architect of the twentieth (or of any other) century. Born in 1869, he was almost the exact contemporary of Frank Lloyd Wright and Charles Rennie Mackintosh, with both of whom he had something in common. A largely self-taught designer with a profound intuitive grasp of three-dimensional form, Lutyens had started his career by designing modern romantic vernacular country villas for the Edwardian *nouveau-riche* before embracing and then developing what he called the 'High Game' of Renaissance Classicism. Part of a generation of architects who had reacted impatiently against the stylistic eclecticism and sentimental associationism of the Victorians in favour of the Grand Manner, he demonstrated an ability to handle the Classical language with rare and conspicuous originality. His talent was recognised even by government, for Lutyens was first asked to design the new capital of British India at New Delhi and then, not long after, the Cenotaph in Whitehall, the national memorial to the million British Empire dead of the Great War. This, with its subtle optical corrections or *entasis* (the slight curving of surfaces) and severe abstracted forms, is an example of what Christopher Hussey, Lutyens's first biographer, described as his 'Elemental Mode'.

The Thiepval arch is another example of this Elemental

Mode, but one in which Lutyens explored the geometrical possibilities and structural logic of the Roman triumphal arch form. With its monumental mass governed by Lutyens's treatment of set-backs or recessions on alternate sides as the structure rises, and with its shape given added dynamism by the walls sloping back at a greater angle at higher levels, it proclaims Lutyens's belief in the timelessness and resonance of the Classical language. 'My generation is – perhaps I ought to say was – a humanist generation,' he wrote in 1931. 'We believed that the measure of man's architecture was man, and that the rhythm of a building should correspond to the rhythms familiar in human life.' How appropriate, therefore, that the most powerful executed expression of that humanist tradition he had embraced should have been to proclaim the importance of human life in war, in death. That nine decades later, in a very different cultural climate, the Memorial to the Missing continues to move, and awe, the visitor testifies to the continuing potency of Lutyens's architectural vision.

Perhaps the greatest puzzle is that such a monument of transcendent genius should have been commissioned by the government of a nation notorious for its indifference towards works of art combined with great reluctance to pay for them. For once, official architecture was great architecture, and a state that had shown shocking indifference to the scale of casualties during the war made some recompense by constructing cemeteries and memorials of remarkable beauty and artistic quality. Indeed, the work of the Imperial War Graves Commission between the world wars constitutes both the largest and the most inspired programme of public design ever completed by a British government agency, despite difficult and worsening economic conditions – and this was carried out overseas. Rudyard Kipling called it 'The biggest single bit of work since any of the Pharaohs – and they only worked in their own country.'

It may seem a paradox that the cataclysm of the Great War which so damaged European civilisation should also have generated works of art. Today, that long struggle is often exclusively understood through the medium of the poetry, writing and painting that it generated. For the British, the horror and futility of the conflict is interpreted through the verse of Wilfred Owen, Siegfried Sassoon and Edmund Blunden and through the memoirs or novels of Robert Graves, Henry Williamson, Sassoon and many more. Visually, its destructiveness and barbarism are imagined as much through the canvases of the best of the official war artists – Paul Nash, C. R. W. Nevinson, Stanley Spencer and William Orpen – as from the familiar photographs of the squalor of the trenches or the desolation of Passchendaele. The Imperial War Museum, indeed, arguably contains the greatest collection of twentieth-century British painting. What is seldom mentioned in this context is architecture, and sculpture. Yet the losses of the war gave rise to memorials which are artistic creations of a high order: the Cenotaph and the Artillery Memorial in London, for instance, and some of the cemeteries and Memorials to the Missing created by the War Graves Commission (to say nothing of the memorials produced by the Italians, Germans and others).

It is often assumed, with some justice, that the death toll and trauma of the Great War, by discrediting the attitudes, traditions and systems which allowed it to be pursued for so long, and so ruthlessly, ensured the subsequent rise to dominance of modernism in the arts. Yet, in fact, that war generated in the subsequent memorials a late but vital flowering of the European Classical tradition in architecture, if for a terrible purpose. And of all the Commission's memorials to the half-million British 'Missing' of the Great War, the most intellectually distinguished, the most astonishing and powerful, is the complex composition of arches raised overlooking the Ancre near where the old village and *château* of Thiepval once stood and where so very many suffered violent deaths. How curious, but how significant, that one of the finest works of British architecture of the twentieth century should stand not in Britain itself but on the opposite side of the English Channel, in rural Picardy, not far from Crécy and Agincourt.

I

....

THE BATTLE OF THE SOMME

The Great War was certainly a world war: a dozen nations were involved and fighting took place on the Eastern Front in Poland and Russia, in the foothills of the Alps in Italy, in the Balkans, in Turkey, Palestine and Arabia, in the Caucasus and Mesopotamia, even in parts of Africa as well as on the high seas all over the globe. But for the British, the historical imagination is dominated by the Western Front, where the invading German armies struggled against the armies of the British, French and Belgians and where most British casualties occurred. In particular, the British remain haunted by the huge casualties squandered to achieve small territorial gains first at the Battle of the Somme in 1916 and then at the Third Battle of Ypres, better known as Passchendaele, the following year. Both remain deeply controversial campaigns, as does the associated decision to wage a bloody war of attrition against Imperial Germany. There is already a vast, and growing, literature on the First World War in the West, and on the Battle of the Somme in particular, so that no more than a summary of events is given here.

The Great War started at the beginning of August 1914. The causes have been endlessly debated, but mobilisation by the armies of the Austro-Hungarian Empire, Russia, Germany and France was a response to deep-seated tensions both within and between these states which were exacerbated by a system of treaties and alliances, by military rivalry and by nationalist feeling. The catalyst was the assassination of the Archduke Franz Ferdinand, heir to the Austrian throne, on 28 June. As far as the British were concerned, it was the German violation of the neutrality of Belgium required by the long-prepared Schlieffen Plan for the invasion of France which precipitated the declaration of war on 4 August. What the British war aims were is more difficult to decide, for they changed as time passed and as war fever became entrenched; the war, indeed, soon had a momentum of its own – as the Battle of the Somme demonstrated.

Following the outbreak of war, the German army swept into France through Belgium. The small British Expeditionary Force, immediately sent out to assist the French, was obliged to retreat from Mons in Belgium. The German intention was to threaten Paris and defeat France in six weeks, but the advance was halted by the French on the river Marne. The Germans then retreated to the Aisne, and there followed 'The Race to the Sea': a series of manoeuvres by each side to outflank the other to the north-east. The German attempt to seize the crucial ports on the English Channel was defeated by the British defence of the old Flemish city of Ypres. Because of the deadly efficiency of modern firepower, with artillery and machine guns, combined with a lack of mobility, casualties in the campaigns of 1914 were unprecedentedly huge. Both sides dug in and by the end of the year vast armies faced each other from defensive positions along lines of trenches stretching some 450 miles across Belgium and France from the English Channel to the Swiss frontier.

In 1915, all the nations geared up for what was clearly going to be a long and bloody struggle. Gas was used as a weapon for the first time, and attempts at breaking the defensive trench lines resulted in large casualties for little gain, with the British in particular being involved in bloody campaigns at Neuve-Chapelle, Loos and Ypres. Meanwhile, the small surviving professional British army in Belgium and France, which had suffered huge casualties, was being augmented by the volunteers who had responded to Kitchener's appeal – two million had come forward in six months, inspired by a great wave of patriotic ardour. It was not, however, until the following year that this large 'New Army' would be committed to a major battle.

The French were anxious that the British army should launch an offensive, particularly after the Germans launched their own offensive on the French at Verdun in February 1916. Haig, who had replaced Sir John French as commander-in-chief in December 1915, planned to do this in Flanders, but Joffre, the French chief of staff, wanted it to be a joint campaign and insisted on launching an offensive either side of the river Somme, where the British and French armies met. North of the Somme, up the valley of the Ancre, British troops had replaced the French in the front line in the late summer of 1915. This was a section of the front that had seen little serious action since the fighting of 1914, and for good reason. Almost everywhere, the Germans occupied the high ground and had prepared three separate lines of defence. Every village and every spur and vantage point was heavily fortified and defended with machine-gun emplacements while the dry chalk ground was ideal for constructing deep bunkers, massively reinforced with concrete, which were almost impervious to artillery fire. Dug-outs along the east bank of the Ancre, built by Russian prisoners, were large and up to forty feet deep. As Lyn Macdonald has written, 'If the German command had been able to choose a single stretch of their five-hundred-mile front on which to beat an Allied offensive, they would have chosen to meet it on the Somme where their line was virtually impregnable.' What, with hindsight, seems clear is the sheer stupidity of the Battle of the Somme; it should not have been fought in the first place and, after its disastrous beginning, should never have been continued.

The Allied offensive was planned for the end of June, by which time it had become largely a British effort owing to the dreadful losses the French were suffering in the 'mincing-machine' of Verdun. Only three French divisions were now allotted to the offensive on the Somme while there were nineteen British divisions: the new Fourth Army under the command of General Sir Henry Rawlinson. The British occupied the line north of Maricourt and the offensive was to be along a front of not much more than a dozen miles terminating beyond Beaumont-Hamel to the north. Despite the failures of the previous year, Haig planned a frontal assault to break the German lines and to allow the cavalry to operate in the open country beyond, along the line of the old straight Roman road north-east from Albert to Bapaume. This assault was to be preceded by a massive and sustained artillery bombardment to destroy the German defences and, thus, to allow the Allied troops virtually to walk across no man's land and take possession of the enemy's trench system. A diversionary attack was also planned further north, at Gommecourt, but this had no effect on the German troop dispositions. Indeed, the Germans were well aware of the elaborate preparations being made behind the British front line – the area between Albert and Amiens was made into a vast British armed camp – and were fully expecting an attack.

The success of the 'Big Push' would depend on meticulous timing, with a 'creeping barrage' moving ahead of the advancing British troops. Objectives and schedules were all carefully planned in advance. Because the New Army was comparatively untrained, and certainly largely unfamiliar with the ghastly reality of trench warfare, the soldiers were ordered to adhere strictly to the prescribed tactics and to advance continuously in lines. As the British Army training manual insisted, 'The men must learn to obey by instinct without thinking. The whole advance must be carried out as a drill.' Despite the reservations of Rawlinson and others, it was decided that 'The assaulting troops must push forward at a steady pace in successive lines, each line adding fresh impetus to the preceding line.'

The British artillery bombardment began on 24 June. Almost three million shells had been brought forward ready to feed 1,000 field guns, 180 heavy guns and 245 heavy howitzers. The barrage was spectacular and relentless; the effect on the German defenders terrifying and demoralising as they sheltered deep below ground, deafened and shell-shocked by the unceasing explosions. Their deep and well-designed bunkers were not, however, destroyed by the shelling and, in truth, the British artillery was neither efficient nor accurate. Worse, the barbed wire defences in front of the German trenches remained largely uncut by the shelling. Furthermore, the German counter-batteries were not much damaged by the bombardment and returned shell for shell, causing heavy casualties in the British front line even before the advance began. Originally, the assault was planned for 28 June but it was postponed until 1 July owing to bad weather, and two more days of shelling ensued while the first line of troops had to remain most uncomfortably in forward positions.

The morning of Saturday, 1 July, began with ground mist but turned into a fine summer's day. Zero hour was 7.30 a.m. This was preceded by a final thunderous artillery barrage and the detonation of large mines which had been placed at certain points under the German front line. Every man was given a tot of strong Navy rum. Then the whistle blew and the British troops climbed out of the trenches and, encumbered by equipment weighing 60 pounds, began to walk eastwards, uphill, towards the enemy. So began what one survivor described as 'the opening of the Battle of the Somme, the most violent and ruthless battle in the history of the world'. Its outcome would depend on who reached the parapet of the German front line of trenches first: the British, ready to throw grenades down any bunkers in which the defenders may have survived; or the Germans, unable to retreat, emerging, shell-shocked, from their dug-outs when the shelling stopped, and fighting for their lives, to take up their defensive positions. In a few places, usually where officers disobeyed orders and used unorthodox tactics, the German line was seized and temporarily held, but most of the advancing lines of British infantry never reached their objectives. Indeed, most of the dead were killed on ground already held before the advance began.

What happened on 1 July 1916 to the north and south of Thiepval has been described and analysed countless times. The British artillery barrage was lifted too soon so that the German defenders were able to rush out of their shelters and deploy their machine guns while their artillery batteries continued to devastate the battlefield. The resulting slaughter is recalled in many harrowing testimonies by survivors. Two will suffice here. A sergeant with the 3rd Tyneside Irish remembered seeing, 'away to my left and right, long lines of men. Then I heard the "patter, patter" of machine guns in the distance. By the time I'd gone another ten yards there seemed to be only a few men left around me; by the time I had gone twenty yards, I seemed to be on my own. Then I was hit myself.' F. P. Crozier, commanding the Belfast battalion of the Royal Irish Rifles, later wrote how he saw 'rows upon rows of British soldiers lying dead, dying or wounded, in no man's land. Here and there I see an officer urging on his followers. Occasionally I can see the hands thrown up and then a body flops to the ground. The bursting shells and smoke make visibility poor, but I see enough to convince me that Thiepval village is still held, for it is now 8 a.m. and by 7.45 a.m. it should have fallen […].'

'At 7.30 a.m. the hurricane of shells ceased as suddenly as it had begun,' ran a German account of the morning. 'Our men at once clambered up the steep shafts leading from the dug-outs to daylight and ran for the nearest shell craters. The machine-guns were pulled out of the dug-outs and hurriedly placed in position […]. The advance rapidly crumpled under the hail of shells and bullets. All along the line men could be seen throwing up their arms into the air and collapsing never to rise again. […] The noise of battle became indescribable. The shouting of orders and the shrill British cheers as they charged forward could be heard above the violent and intense fusillade of machine-guns and the bursting bombs, and above the deep thundering of the artillery and the shell explosions. With all this were mingled the moans and groans of the wounded, the cries for help and the last screams of death. Again and again the extended lines of British infantry broke against the German defences like waves against a cliff, only to be beaten back. It was an amazing spectacle of unexampled gallantry, courage and bull-dog determination on both sides.'

That dreadful day ended in chaos and confusion, but it soon emerged that a catastrophe had occurred. Not only was the German line not broken, but a fifth of the 100,000 men who had advanced into no man's land did not return. British casualties on that first day amounted to a total of about 60,000. The precise figures are: 19,240 dead and 35,493 wounded, with 2,152 missing and 585 taken prisoner. It was the greatest loss of life in British military history. German casualties were about a tenth of the British. Furthermore, it has been estimated that perhaps a third of those killed or who went missing on 1 July died from wounds from which they might have survived if treated, but many of the wounded remained isolated on the battlefield for hours and, in some cases for two and even three days, despite the Germans offering a humanitarian truce at times along many sections of the front.

Even ninety years on, reading of these events can induce feelings of anger, and shame, that such things could have happened, and there has been much criticism of the tactics employed on the Somme and elsewhere by the British high command. But, as John Keegan has written, 'The simple truth of 1914–18 trench warfare is that the massing of large numbers of soldiers unprotected by anything but cloth uniforms, however they were trained, however equipped, against large masses of other soldiers, protected by earthworks and barbed wire and provided with rapid fire weapons, was bound to result in very heavy casualties among the attackers. [...] The basic and stark fact [...] was that the conditions of warfare between 1914 and 1918 predisposed towards slaughter and that only an entirely different technology, one not available until a generation later, could have averted such an outcome.'

Even so, the fact remains that the French 6th Army under Marshall Fayolle, south of Maricourt, achieved all their objectives on 1 July and with fewer casualties proportionally. Lieut.-Col. C. O. Head later wrote that, 'For a long time I fought alongside, that is, actually adjoining, the French on the Somme, so had some opportunity of comparing their methods and performances with ours. While we struggled painfully through the mud, they progressed in clean jumps, and finally got far ahead of us across the Bapaume–Péronne Road, while we never got within a mile of it. Our weight of metal was heavier than theirs, our men and regimental officers at least as good: why was there such a discrepancy in our performances?' The military historian Basil Liddell Hart, who had himself fought on the Somme, quoted in his own account of the world war an Australian officer, J. A. Raws, writing, shortly before his own death in battle, of the 'murder' of many of his friends 'through the incompetence, callousness, and personal vanity of those high in authority'.

Because communications had broken down and because of the confusion, it took time for the enormity of the catastrophe of 1 July to penetrate the minds of the British high command (and it has often been observed how remote the red-tabbed staff officers were from the actual conditions in the trenches: the commander-in-chief's headquarters was in the *château* at Beauquesne, fifteen miles behind the front). The following day, Haig believed that the enemy 'has undoubtedly been severely shaken and he has few reserves in hand', which was not, of course, the case. The German high command was, however, alarmed at the scale of the British attack and brought in an expert on defence, Colonel von Lossberg, who reorganised the Somme front and constructed defence in depth, with a thinly held front line which could always be retaken by counter-attacks if lost. This ensured that the continuation of the battle would be a long and desperate struggle.

Originally, Haig had envisaged a fourteen-day campaign and had agreed that the offensive should be abandoned if success was not achieved. He now proposed to shift the attack to his preferred theatre in Flanders, but Joffre, to whom he had been instructed to defer by the government, insisted that the Somme offensive be continued. On 4 July Haig named Pozières as the chief objective and proclaimed the necessity of 'continuing operations relentlessly and allowing the enemy no respite'. From now on, the Battle of the Somme would be a war of attrition. There is evidence that the British authorities were actually prepared to bear up to 500,000 casualties in this campaign, although in the event Haig did not need to score that high. Sir Douglas Haig was undoubtedly an efficient military technician, as he proved in organising the huge human and material effort required to mount the campaign. Whether he had ability as a tactician was another matter. 'The successful generals of the First World War, those who did not crack outright or decline gradually into pessimism, were a hard lot,' John Keegan has written, 'as they had to be with the casualty figures accumulating on their desks. Some,

4. Looking up into the principal vaults at Thiepval, where the coffering is adapted from the ancient Buddhist stupa at Sanchi in India, a motif which Lutyens had already used on Viceroy's House in New Delhi.

nevertheless, managed to combine toughness of mind with some striking human characteristic [...]. Haig, in whose public manner and private diaries no concern for human suffering was or is discernible, compensated for his aloofness with nothing whatever of the common touch. He seemed to move through the horrors of the First World War as if guided by some inner voice, speaking of a higher purpose and a personal destiny.'

Haig – once described as 'brilliant to the top of his Army boots' by David Lloyd George – was not going to admit defeat and still hoped for that breakthrough which would enable him to unleash his beloved cavalry. For the rest of July, more assaults were ordered, which eventually succeeded, at huge cost, in taking the small areas of ground and destroyed villages whose names are enshrined in those wreaths inside the Thiepval Memorial: Mametz, Courcelette, Fricourt, Bazentin, High Wood, Morval ... All witnessed acts of great heroism, and of unspeakable brutality – on both sides. Pozières eventually was taken, as was Delville Wood, after a desperate struggle. At least the British were now learning from the failure on 1 July and more effective and more imaginative tactics were being employed. By the end of July, when the British and French had lost over 200,000 men and the Germans some 160,000, the southern part of the Somme front had advanced by about three miles, but had hardly moved at all north of the Ancre.

Remorseless, desperate fighting continued until the middle of November, by which time increasingly wet and cold weather had turned the chalky soil into glutinous mud. The Mark I tank, a mechanised armoured vehicle first developed by the British and able to move over barbed wire and trenches, was used for the first time in battle on the Somme front on 15 September. Although tanks were only deployed in limited numbers and not properly used to advantage, the psychological effect they achieved was immense. Thiepval itself, so strongly fortified and so stubbornly defended, finally fell on 26 September, partly owing to the appearance of British tanks outside the village. The British eventually occupied the high ground, but the advance continued so that by the time Haig at last declared the campaign over, on 18 November – shortly after the final capture of Beaumont-Hamel to the north after many attempts – much of the British front line was again down in a valley. The army then had to endure a particularly severe winter in disgusting conditions in flooded trenches.

The Battle of the Somme had achieved gains of some six or seven miles of pulverised, muddy territory and destroyed villages on the southern part of the front. Bapaume remained in German hands. Denis Winter has written that 'a battle fought from July to November 1916 saw the British and German armies fire thirty million shells at each other and suffer a million casualties between them in an area just seven miles square. This staggering fact reveals that no other battlefield in the Great War witnessed more killing per square yard.' The German army was undoubtedly worn down and gravely damaged by the offensive, but whether that compensated for the Allied losses and the unspeakable suffering and dehumanising behaviour engendered on both sides is another matter. Michael Howard has written that 'Since the object of the attack had always been unclear – Haig's expectation of a breakthrough had never been shared by his subordinate commanders – the Allies claimed a victory in terms of attrition.

Indeed they, like their German adversaries, could see no other way of winning the war.'

But even if it is accepted that a policy of prodigal attrition, of a balance of killing, maintained by military and political leaders is acceptable in a supposedly civilised, democratic and Christian society, it was a policy that failed. As Niall Ferguson has concluded, 'The reality was that at best, if one accepts the British official figure for German casualties of 680,000, the Somme was a draw (the British lost 419,654 casualties, the French 204,253). If, as is more likely, the German figure for casualties was correct (450,000), then the strategy of attrition was self-defeating.' The scale of casualties on the Somme was not, in fact, any greater than those suffered by the French, Germans, Austrians and Russians in earlier campaigns, particularly in those on the Eastern Front. What made the losses unbearable for the British public was that they seemed to have been in vain, that no real victory had been gained.

The end of 1916, when the fighting powers had achieved so little after enduring such huge casualties, when European civilisation was tottering, was the moment when a negotiated peace might have been possible, but this was undermined by ambitious politicians and relentlessly confident military leaders as well as by the war fever and hatreds whipped up in each and every nation. And then, four months after the end of the Somme campaign, in March 1917, the Germans rendered the Allied sacrifice somewhat superfluous by suddenly withdrawing some twenty miles to a shorter line of defences – the Hindenburg Line – prepared months earlier, leaving the intervening country stripped and devastated. This tactical retreat was undoubtedly an acknowledgement of weakness, but the new line was even more impregnable than the earlier front on the Somme and Ancre. For the remainder of that terrible year, 1917, this section of the Western Front was comparatively quiet. British offensives took place at Arras, at Cambrai – where, at last, tanks were used in large numbers and effectively – and, above all, in Flanders. Here, between July and November, Haig ordered an advance which was officially called the Third Battle of Ypres, another bloody campaign of attrition, which is better known by the name of the stinking muddy hell of Passchendaele. It was described by Lloyd George – who had succeeded Asquith as Prime Minister in 1916 and who never had the courage to dismiss his problematic commander-in-chief – as 'the battle which, with the Somme and Verdun, will always rank as the most gigantic, tenacious, grim, futile and bloody fight ever waged in the history of war'.

In 1918, Imperial Germany made a last, brilliant but desperate attempt to win the war by military means before the advent of American troops – the United States had entered the fight the previous year – would tip the balance of power irrevocably in favour of the Allies. Reinforced by many divisions from the East, available now that both Russia and Roumania were out of the fight, Ludendorff, the *de facto* German commander-in-chief under Hindenburg, succeeded where Haig and all the other generals had failed and smashed through the fortified lines of trenches. A massive offensive launched on 21 March on a wide fifty-mile front south of Arras achieved complete tactical and strategic surprise. Using short and devastating artillery barrages and units of storm troops which pressed ahead without bothering to overcome pockets of resistance, the British defences were routed. In just three days, all the territory gained at such vast human cost in 1916 was recaptured. Even Albert, which had always been behind the British lines – and whose shell-damaged basilica with a statue of the Virgin and Child hanging precariously from the top of the tower was a prominent wartime landmark – was taken. On 9 April a further successful German assault was launched in Flanders and, two days later, Haig – who had been so confident that his war of attrition was defeating the German army – issued his desperate order of the day: 'There is no other course open to us but to fight it out. Every position must be held to the last man: there must be no retirement. With our backs to the wall and believing in the justice of our cause each one of us must fight on to the end.'

By this stage, however, the tide was turning. The German advance on Amiens was stopped by the Australians at Villers-Bretonneux and Ludendorff's offensive was faltering. This was partly because of Germany's economic exhaustion, which became painfully evident to her troops when the overrun trenches were found to be well stocked with food and provisions. A war of movement now followed as the Allied armies – now under Foch as supreme commander-in-chief – counter-attacked and steadily pushed the German forces back, taking many thousands of prisoners. Having learnt from the success of Ludendorff's own tactics, the French counter-attack on the Marne on 18 July was followed by a massive assault on 8 August largely by Australians and Canadians, backed with tanks. The liberation of Albert – its basilica now reduced to rubble by British shelling – and the old Somme battlefields soon followed. Ludendorff described 8 August as 'the black day of the German army in the history of the war' and realised that the fighting had to end. As the Allied blockade of the Central Powers was causing much suffering and starvation back home, the morale of the German army was beginning to collapse. With Bulgaria and Turkey both out of the fight and the Austro-Hungarian Empire disintegrating, Germany – even though its armies had yet to be driven back out of France and Belgium to its own frontiers – was now threatened by revolution at home and asked for an armistice. It took effect on the eleventh hour of the eleventh day of the eleventh month of 1918. The war to end all wars was finally over – at least in the West, for fighting continued in Russia and elsewhere in the East.

....

2

WAR MEMORIALS

Perhaps as many as ten million died in the Great War, both soldiers and civilians. A war which was as unnecessary as it was tragic and yet was pursued with ruthless vigour by governments left a legacy of rancour and hatred. The physical legacy, of devastated countryside and destroyed towns and villages, eventually healed, but the human loss could not be restored. Perhaps little more than the casualty figures are necessary to begin to understand the subsequent unhappy history of the twentieth century. Britain and her Dominions lost a million dead, France 1,700,000, Italy 460,000, Germany two million, the Austro-Hungarian Empire 1,500,000, Russia perhaps 1,700,000 while the figure for Turkey is unknown. Casualty rates were higher among officers, and something like one in three of all young men who were between nineteen and twenty-two years of age when war began were killed. Even among those who survived, many subsequently died of their wounds or from being gassed. Many more were left blinded or mutilated, unable to work or function, while populations all over Europe were left unhappily unbalanced in terms of sex and age.

The loss to the British Empire was 1,104,890 dead – English, Scots, Welsh, Irish, Canadians, Australians, New Zealanders, South Africans, Indians, and more. Such figures transcend ordinary human comprehension, so that, in a contemporary Armistice Day broadcast, a visual metaphor was used to indicate the scale of the nation's loss: that is, if all the men of the British Empire who were killed between 1914 and 1918 were to have marched together in rows of four to the Cenotaph, when the front of the column arrived in Whitehall its tail would still be at Durham. The consequences of this loss and trauma in terms of politics, religion, social behaviour and the arts would take time to emerge, at least in Britain. Soon, the Modern Movement would demand an entirely new, non-historical architecture to serve a new, better society. The immediate need, however, was to make sense of the sacrifice by honouring the dead. For in the context of Judaeo-Christian humanist civilisation as it had so far evolved, and comforted by the fact of ultimate victory, every individual who had died was now considered worthy of commemoration.

There was a huge demand for memorials during the decade after 1918; as David Cannadine has written, 'inter-war Britain was probably more obsessed with death than any other period of modern history'. For the architect, the sculptor, the monumental mason and the letter-cutter, therefore, it was a very busy period. Every church, every school, every village and town in Britain soon had a memorial – a tablet, a free-standing cross or, perhaps, a bronze statue of a steel-helmeted Tommy on a pedestal – listing the names of those who enlisted and never returned. But for cities and for the state's official response to the casualty lists, something more considered, more monumental, more architectural, was required. And to this challenge, the architectural profession in Britain rose with, on the whole, conspicuous success. Indeed, in terms of the design of war memorials, the Great War occurred at exactly the right time for, thanks to the revival of Classicism and the enthusiasm for the Grand Manner in the two decades before 1914, there were many architects able and willing to attempt the monumental. This would not have been the case in the Late Victorian period (as the general sentimental mediocrity of Boer War memorials suggests), while after the Second World War an enfeebled Classical tradition was sustained by the example of what Lutyens and others had achieved after the First.

The war memorial – one that commemorated not a victory or a victorious commander but human sacrifice – was a comparatively new conception which had emerged in the previous century. For inspiration, designers had to look to the distant past, to ancient Egypt, Greece and Rome, as well as to the Italian Renaissance. The obvious precedents were the pyramid, the obelisk, the column, the triumphal arch and the temple. While monarchs and national leaders had been celebrated by the equestrian statue on a pedestal, few such monumental architectural forms had been permanently created in Britain. Indeed, before the Great War, Great Britain erected no significant national war memorials. There is no single national monument commemorating the Boer War but only local and regimental memorials. The same is true of the Crimean War, for the handsome monument by John Bell in Waterloo Place is only for the Regiment of Guards. Even the great quarter-century-long struggle with the French which was finally concluded at Waterloo gave rise to no national memorial, neither in London nor elsewhere.

This was not for want of trying, but the projects by, say, John Martin for a memorial at the top of Portland Place or Thomas Harrison's design for a 'National Building' to record

5. Lutyens's All-India War Memorial arch in New Delhi: a creative development of the Arc de Triomphe theme whose internal walls bear the names of 13,516 Indian Army soldiers.

British victories in painting and sculpture on a quay by the Thames – a sort of Valhalla – remained on paper. It took two decades for the government to celebrate Nelson with a giant column in a new square named after his final victory, while the name of Wellington's victory was only applied to a new street and a fine new bridge across the Thames. A marble-clad arch on the Roman model celebrating military victories was designed by Nash as an entrance to Buckingham Palace, but later had to be moved to the corner of Hyde Park. The contrast with the Paris of Napoleon is marked; well might John Timbs complain in 1868 that 'London differs essentially from many other European capitals in the paucity of its Arches, or ornamental gateways.' Scotland did at least attempt to raise a replica of the Parthenon as a National Monument to her dead in the French Wars on Calton Hill in Edinburgh, but then neglected to complete it.

Although Renaissance Italian cities and Louis XIV's France had occasionally indulged in memorials and statues on the Imperial Roman model, the modern monumental memorial to a war or to a cause was first given characteristic form in late-eighteenth-century France and early-nineteenth-century Germany. In France, E.-L. Boullée proposed vast, abstract and monumental structures dedicated to vague and incipiently totalitarian ideals, while similarly simplified antique forms were composed on a monumental scale in Friedrich Gilly's unbuilt but influential proposal for a monument to Frederick the Great in Berlin. In Revolutionary and Napoleonic France, as in Prussia, all resources were increasingly mobilised by the state and the army was glorified and almost worshipped – so that Paris not only has the Arc de Triomphe but also the church of the Madeleine, originally built as a temple dedicated to the Grande Armée.

In the German states and in Russia, as in France, military and national memorials were erected which looked back to pre-Christian antiquity, to the temples and funeral monuments of Greece and to the columns and triumphal arches of Rome. After the defeat of Napoleon, two astonishing monuments were raised in Bavaria overlooking the Danube near Regensburg. One was the Walhalla, inspired by the Parthenon, the other the circular Befreiungshalle or Hall of Liberation, an extraordinary abstract Neo-Classical conception; both were designed by Leo von Klenze, who also enhanced Munich with a Greek propylaeum and stoa. Later, after the Unification of Germany in 1871, the Siegessäule was raised in Berlin, a giant granite victory column rising from a circular temple and encrusted with captured cannon to celebrate the successive defeats of Denmark, Austria and France. This tendency culminated in the huge and rugged Völkerschlachtdenkmal or peoples' struggle monument in Leipzig, a colossal and intimidating structure by Bruno Schmitz completed in 1913 to celebrate the centenary of the 'Battle of the Nations' in which the forces of Napoleon were defeated.

All these memorials and many more, both ancient and modern, were discussed and illustrated in a series of articles by A. E. Richardson and R. Randal Phillips published in the *Architectural Review* soon after the outbreak of war in 1914. Not surprisingly, given the context as well as the francophilia of much Edwardian architecture, the Napoleonic monuments and memorials were recommended for emulation while the authors were obliged to condemn the more recent and brutally monumental precedents furnished by Imperial Germany. London, they felt, was not yet worthy of comparison with Paris in the matter of memorials, and they concluded that 'at the close of the War the nation will demand the erection of a national memorial to the memory of her fallen sons. There must be no niggardly dealing in connection with it. Isolated statues and mediocre tablets will not suffice to reward the terrific nature of the struggle and its all-important effect on the destiny of the race. We are too close to the scene at present to estimate its character, but when the time comes for the consideration of a national monument the thing must be undertaken in a spirit of greatness.'

British architects were, however, now reasonably well equipped to rise to the occasion, as they would not have been a half-century before. The Gothic Revival and the Arts and Crafts movement that it engendered – the tradition from which Lutyens himself emerged – had been a vital and creative force in Britain, but it began to be appreciated that it had not produced an architecture suitable for an imperial city, fit for the heart of the British Empire. Since about 1890, architects had rediscovered the English Renaissance Classicism of Inigo Jones and Sir Christopher Wren, and produced an ebullient commercial and civic architecture which we call Edwardian Baroque. After that, they began to explore the whole European Classical tradition so that by the time war broke out a monumental Classicism was in vogue with the leaders of the profession and was being refined by a younger generation. What was lacking, however, were the opportunities for the monumental civic gesture at home, for they seemed only to occur abroad: in India and South Africa, with New Delhi and the Union Buildings at Pretoria.

Indeed it was in South Africa – where, perhaps significantly, the British war on the independent Boer republics had been nationalistic and ruthless – rather than in Britain, that the first war memorials were raised and provided the only immediate precedents for those built after 1918. Under the influence of Cecil Rhodes, Herbert Baker looked to Rome and to Agrigentum for his austere and powerful design for the Kimberley Memorial, and then to Greece for his memorial to Rhodes himself on the side of Table Mountain above Cape Town. And Lutyens, who travelled to South Africa in 1910 to design the Johannesburg Art Gallery, followed with his Rand Regiments Memorial in the same city, a prophetic design in which he first explored the possibilities of the triumphal arch theme. The Roman arch might seem an inappropriate form for a memorial to the dead as it was in origin a celebration of military victory, but a precedent had already been set for the use of the arch as a war memorial in the United States after the Civil War.

Back in Britain, the architectural mood in the years before the Great War can be gauged by two influential books, both published in 1914. One was Geoffrey Scott's *Architecture of Humanism*, a defence of the architecture of the Italian Renaissance and Baroque against the moralising strictures of Ruskin and the Arts and Crafts movement; the other was A. E. Richardson's *Monumental Classic Architecture in Great Britain and Ireland during the XVIIIth & XIXth Centuries*, which, with the help of magnificent plates, looked again at the long-despised Neo-Classicism of Adam, Chambers, Soane and Cockerell. Such tastes were already reflected in the new architectural schools, which were influenced by the Beaux-Arts system in France. Particularly important here was the Liverpool School of Architecture under C. H. Reilly, which promoted an austere modern Neo-Classicism and at which such Beaux-Arts-inspired projects as 'A Mausoleum' or 'A Monument to a Naval Hero' were regularly set. One student, H. Chalton Bradshaw, produced a design for a mausoleum which was clearly inspired by both Baker's Rhodes Memorial and Schmitz's monument at Leipzig, and in 1913 he became the first Rome Scholar in Architecture, winning a new prize which enabled him to study in Italy. Bradshaw is significant because, although gassed and wounded, he would survive the war to win two competitions for Memorials to the Missing – at Ploegsteert and Louverval – as well as designing the Guards Memorial by St James's Park. He, like so many of his contemporaries, was well trained to deal with the architectural consequences of mass slaughter.

Once the conflict began in 1914 and the nature of the struggle became clear through the long casualty lists, endless proposals for national war memorials in London were made. In these, the monumental Classical theme was inevitably dominant. Ideas for triumphal arches and memorial halls, often combined with grand town planning schemes, were published. Reginald Blomfield and Sir Aston Webb, for instance, proposed replacing the Charing Cross railway bridge with a new monumental war memorial bridge with triumphal arches at either end. Another idea, which was taken up officially and which eventually came to fruition in a very different manner in the old Bethlem Hospital near Waterloo Station, was for a national war museum combined with a 'Hall of Honour' to be built in Hyde Park. Lutyens prepared sketch designs for this in 1917. The following year, in August 1918, he made a design for a temporary War Shrine, again to be built in Hyde Park, of plaster, to replace an even more temporary shrine (*not* by Lutyens) erected at the expense of Messrs Waring & Gillow to mark the fourth anniversary of the outbreak of war (this was popular, although Siegfried Sassoon, on leave from the Front, thought it 'an outburst of national vulgarity [...] one of our insults to the dead'). In several respects, Lutyens's proposal anticipated his executed designs for the Imperial War Graves Commission as it envisaged an altar or 'War Stone' flanked by open square pylons topped by pine cones. The design was criticised for its deliberate lack of Christian symbolism and this, combined with the encouraging progress of the war, led to its being shelved.

With the war over, more grand schemes for a national war memorial were produced and committees established to consider the problem. In the event, however, London was not to gain any more triumphal arches and the national memorial was to be a comparatively modest structure, originally intended only to be temporary: the Cenotaph. Perhaps that is rather typical of England. When the Prime Minister, Lloyd George, needed to find 'some prominent artist' to design a temporary, nondenominational 'catafalque' for the Peace Celebrations planned for 19 July 1919, Lutyens was recommended by Sir Alfred Mond, First Commissioner of Works. The legend is that Lutyens produced a sketch of his proposal for Sir Frank Baines, chief architect to the Office of Works, in ten minutes, but in fact he had been thinking about it for some time and had already explored the idea of a pylon supporting a funeral effigy in his design for the Southampton war memorial. Now the recumbent effigy was replaced by a symbolic coffin or sarcophagus on top of a tall pylon to be erected in the middle of Whitehall. The concept was converted into

6. 'The people's shrine': the temporary Cenotaph in Whitehall piled high with wreaths and flowers after the Peace Celebrations held on 19 July 1919.

wood and plaster in a matter of days. And then, the generals and politicians and soldiers having marched past, something unexpected happened: the temporary structure became sacred, 'the people's shrine'. Tens of thousands of women, grieving for husbands or boyfriends or sons who were buried abroad or who had simply disappeared, found that Lutyens had created a visible focus for mourning. A mountain of flowers and wreaths piled up around it; and a million people made pilgrimage. Eventually, the government acceded to what Lutyens called 'the human sentiment of millions' and allowed the Cenotaph to be replicated permanently in stone the following year.

The Cenotaph speaks through pure form and deep cultural resonances. This slim pylon, which makes no attempt to compete with the height of the surrounding government buildings, somehow managed to express the inarticulate grief of a wounded, damaged society. As, later, at Thiepval, Lutyens knew better than to resort to tendentious symbolism, whether religious, or national or military. Words and symbols were not required, although there are in fact words carved on it – just three: 'THE GLORIOUS DEAD', even though the fate of most of them was not necessarily glorious. Not that the Cenotaph is simple; it is a highly sophisticated essay in geometry and form. The bulk diminishes as it rises, governed by Lutyens's own personal system of massing, with set-backs on alternate faces, while all the verticals and horizontals are not straight lines at all but subtle curves, governed by a system of *entasis* or optical correction employed in ancient Greek temples to give visual dynamism – what Christopher Hussey called its 'magic quality'. All the verticals are curved and sloped so that they would converge at an imaginary point some nine hundred feet in the air (the 'frightful calculations' for this *entasis* are said to have filled a manuscript book of thirty-three pages). In its abstraction, the Cenotaph might seem somehow 'modern', but its power comes through it being rooted in a tradition which had – and still has – resonance: the Classical, Renaissance tradition – hence its success, and the call for it to be permanent. And so perfect is the Cenotaph for its purpose that, after a second world war, nothing more was needed than to carve two more dates into the Portland stone: '1939–1945'.

The Cenotaph is remarkable for the absence of any visible emblems or symbols on it representing Triumph, or Heroism, or Victory; there are only carved wreaths and ribbons, and three flags along each flank. It speaks only of death, and loss. Nor are there any religious symbols: there is no cross, let alone a crucifix, nor representations of angels, of St George or St Michael in armour. This is, perhaps, surprising in a nation with an established Church. The bishops, indeed, were very unhappy about this and the burial of the Unknown Warrior in Westminster Abbey on Armistice Day 1920, when the permanent Cenotaph was unveiled, was the Church of England's riposte to this official secularism. Stephen Graham later recalled Lutyens saying, 'There was some horror in Church circles. *What!* A pagan monument in the midst of Whitehall! That is why we have a rival shrine in the Abbey, the Unknown Warrior, but even an unknown soldier might not have been a Christian, the more unknown the less sure you could be.'

But the Great War was a conflict in which men of all religions, and none, had been fed into the slaughter. Lutyens knew this and, influenced by Theosophy (owing to his

7. 'Romanticism flowing out of realism under the stress of emotion':
the Scottish National War Memorial by Sir Robert Lorimer on top of
Edinburgh Castle Rock.

independent-minded aristocratic wife, Lady Emily Lytton), argued that not just in Whitehall but in all the war cemeteries and memorials to be built by the Imperial War Graves Commission there should be forms which had meaning 'irrespective of creed or caste'. The matter was debated in Parliament and the massed ranks of bishops, cardinals and ministers, and other supporters of the symbolic Cross (which included Herbert Baker), were defeated. As Lutyens remarked afterwards, it was important 'to make folk realise the inherent cruelty of the *forced* Cross'. That, however, did not deter the *Catholic Herald* from later dismissing the Cenotaph as 'nothing more or less than a pagan monument, insulting to Christianity [...] a disgrace in a so called Christian land' as it was for 'Atheist, Mohammedan, Buddhist, Jew, men of any religion or none'.

What the bishops and clergy, let alone the generals and headmasters and all those who argued for Christian symbolism, might have achieved in London if they had had their way is perhaps suggested by the Scottish National War Memorial, completed on top of Edinburgh Castle Rock in 1927. Here, the Arts and Crafts designer Sir Robert Lorimer converted a barrack block into a shrine, overwhelmingly national and Gothic in character, in which the history of the war and Scotland's dreadful losses – much higher in proportion to the population than England's – is told in sculpture, heraldry and stained glass, with the names of battles and regimental badges carved in stone in the Hall of Honour. Hanging in the arch which leads to the shrine itself is a figure of St Michael, in armour. It is a romantic, and tragic, conception and the mood is military and Christian, even if not explicitly so – in marked contrast to the understated coolness

[45]

of Lutyens's simple white pylon in Whitehall. This was commented on by contemporaries: 'The difference in character between the English and Scottish peoples has never been more clearly shown than by their respective War Memorials,' wrote Hussey. 'It is the difference between inarticulate sentiment, and romanticism flowing out of realism under the stress of emotion. [...] The emotion that makes an Englishman bow his head in silence impels the normally silent Scot to lift up his voice. The Scottish need to unlock their hearts [...].' Attempts to distinguish national character in the two memorials are, however, undermined by the fact that one was ten years in the making while the other was initially conceived in a short space of time as a purely temporary structure. It was, nevertheless, the understated secular and abstract Classical manner of the London memorial which largely governed the work of the War Graves Commission.

As for the other constituent parts of the then United Kingdom, The Welsh Memorial in Cardiff is an open circular Corinthian colonnade enclosing a naked figure of Victory above three servicemen in uniform. Its style was an appropriate response to its site in the centre of Cathays Park, the city's formally planned Edwardian civic quarter, but otherwise it is a disappointingly feeble composition not at all typical of its designer, the church architect Ninian Comper (who was Scots rather than Welsh). For the Irish National War Memorial in Phoenix Park in Dublin – commemorating 49,000 Irishmen, both Protestant and Catholic: all volunteers as conscription was never introduced across the Irish Sea – a memorial garden with pergolas and fountains combined with an abstracted version of a standing cross was chosen after an earlier proposal to erect a memorial in Merrion Square had been rejected by the government of the Irish Free State. This memorial garden was finally completed in 1938; its designer was again Edwin Lutyens, an Englishman with a surname of German origin but whose mother had been born in Killarney.

3

....

THE ARCHITECT

When the permanent Cenotaph was unveiled on Armistice Day, 1920, its designer was fifty-one years old. Thanks to the success of his memorial, Edwin Lutyens was now a national figure, already knighted for his work on New Delhi and for his unpaid advice to the Imperial War Graves Commission. But he was not exactly an establishment figure, and in the changing architectural climate of the following decade, increasingly polarised between so-called traditionalists and modernists, he was never perceived as a reactionary or as blimpish, as were Baker and Blomfield (the latter the author of a book which pilloried what he referred to as *Modernismus*). Lutyens was always admired by the younger generation, however committed they were to modernism. He was happy in the company of the young, as in that of craftsmen and workmen. There was something essentially child-like and irreverent about Lutyens, the 'perennial *enfant terrible*', and his constant patter of (often terrible) puns and jokes infuriated as much as it delighted. His daughter Mary once wrote that 'It has been said of Father that he joked to cover his shyness. That may have been true in his early days but by now it had become a habit and some of his jokes were mere reflexes. For instance, he could never see a dish of butter without exclaiming, "Butter late than never".' Murder has been committed for less, but Lutyens's crippling shyness at public ceremonies and his verbal inarticulateness are well documented, and he seems to have constructed an entertaining character as a form of self-defence as well as a way of seducing potential clients. But much of his humour was conscious and non-verbal, for he was also an inspired caricaturist and cartoonist.

Behind that mask and all the jokes, there was an artist of profound seriousness and absolute integrity. Hussey recounted how, towards the end of his life, Lutyens invited A. S. G. Butler to look at the model of his Liverpool Cathedral and how he 'became as it were transformed and with a kind of anxious humility explained the design [...]. Butler was deeply moved by this first, mid-nocturnal sight of the mighty conception, but more so, he relates, by the appearance of the man beside him, so changed from the eminent, sociable, laughing Lutyens of a few minutes earlier. He saw for those moments the creator, without his protective mask, utterly absorbed and serious, contemplating his greatest creation, humbly, because he saw that it was good.' That great domed cathedral for the Roman Catholics of Liverpool, the drawings for which Lutyens asked to be placed around the walls of his bedroom as he lay dying in 1943, was never to be raised above the skyline overlooking the Mersey to compete with Sir Giles Scott's Gothic tower for the Anglicans, but something of the grandeur and originality of the conception can be grasped when standing under the high vault of the arch at Thiepval.

'One had never seen before, and will never see again, anyone who resembled this singular and delightful man,' Sir Osbert Sitwell recalled. 'An expression of mischievous benevolence was his distinguishing mark, as it was of his work.' By the time it was completed, the architect who could create such an awesomely serious work of art as the Memorial to the Missing of the Somme had become a popular social figure, much in demand for lunch and dinner parties because of his flippant unorthodoxy and humour. Lutyens was of above average height with unusually long legs; John Summerson recorded in 1937 that he was 'a rather big man with a phenomenally round, bald head fixed with wonderful precision on his shoulders. He has small, very blue, provocatively innocent eyes, curiously set; vaguely like portraits of Inigo Jones. He wears a steep butterfly collar and a neat, ordinary tie, and moves with a certain critical, half-humorous deliberation, by no means unimpressive. He smokes absurd little pipes, specially made for him [...]. You rarely see him but in the company of a pack of fans, sniggering at his cracks and wondering what the great Lut will say or do next. Bores all over the Empire hoard his doodles, do their damnedest to collect and recollect some encounter, some passage of wit, wherein they stood irradiated for a moment in the sunshine of authentic Genius.'

Edwin Landseer Lutyens was born in London on 29 March 1869, the ninth son and tenth of the thirteen children of a soldier and inventor turned painter who was descended from Barthold Lütkens, a merchant who had emigrated from Hamburg in the reign of George II. His mother was Irish, the sister of a Governor of Montreal. Unlike his brothers, Ned Lutyens never went to public school and had little formal education. 'Any talent I may have had,' he told Osbert Sitwell, 'was due to a long illness as a boy, which afforded me time to think, and to subsequent ill-health, because I was not allowed to play games, and so had to teach myself, for

8. Lutyens by Meredith Frampton showing 'this singular and delightful man'
as Master of the Art-Workers' Guild in 1933

my enjoyment, to use my eyes instead of my feet. My brothers hadn't the same advantage.' Much of his childhood was spent in the family's second home in Surrey, at Thursley near Godalming, where he would roam the countryside looking at old buildings or at new ones under construction, and visiting builder's yards and watching craftsmen at work, thus acquiring that knowledge of building materials and an awareness of the importance of detail so evident in his own later buildings. According to his daughter, 'He would carry about with him in his wanderings a small pane of clear glass and several pieces of soap sharpened to fine points. Looking through the glass at some detail of a building he wanted to learn about he would trace it with the soap.' By such means did Lutyens develop his acute comprehension of three-dimensional form in terms of walls and roof planes.

Lutyens also had comparatively little architectural education. Captain Lutyens enrolled his sixteen-year-old son at the National Art Training school in South Kensington, but he left after two years and did not finish the course. Now determined to become a 'successful architect', Lutyens became an articled pupil in the busy office of Ernest George and Peto in 1887 (he had really wanted to work in the office of the great Richard Norman Shaw but there was a long waiting list). He stayed for only a year and a half and later claimed he learned nothing there; this was not true, for he absorbed the picturesque vernacular manner of Ernest George, who was a charming artist and – like Shaw – a successful country house builder. It was in this office that Lutyens met the older, public-school-educated Herbert Baker, with whom he went on sketching tours and who much later recalled how his former friend, 'though joking through his short pupillage, quickly absorbed all that was worth learning: he puzzled us at first, but we soon found that he seemed to know by intuition some great truths of our art which were not to be learned there'.

Lutyens set up on his own in 1889 at the age of nineteen – unthinkable today – having received a commission from a family friend to design a small house near Farnham: Crooksbury. This, like most of his early buildings, is in the manner of Ernest George and Norman Shaw and, in truth, is not particularly remarkable, although his first large house, Chinthurst Hill, showed extraordinary promise. Lutyens's work became exceptional only when he began to work for and with his most remarkable client and collaborator, Gertrude Jekyll. Much older than the young architect she befriended, Miss Jekyll was a disciple of Ruskin who had taken up photography as well as painting and had become increasingly interested in gardening as well as in the crafts and traditions of Old West Surrey. When her mother, with whom she lived, died in 1895, Gertrude Jekyll commissioned Lutyens to design Munstead Wood, a new house in a garden she had already established. This was the beginning of a creative collaboration which would last almost forty years. As Mary Lutyens wrote, 'Miss Jekyll knew very little about architecture and Ned even less about gardening. His houses needed gardens and her revolutionary ideas of garden planting and design needed houses. Each found in the other the perfect complement.' A quarter of a century later, Gertrude Jekyll would advise on the planting of the war cemeteries in France.

Lutyens met most of his early clients through Gertrude Jekyll, not least Edward Hudson, the founder and editor of the journal *Country Life*, who assiduously promoted his work. Jealous rivals often assumed Lutyens did so well because of his grand aristocratic marriage, although this was not in fact the case. In 1897, he had married Lady Emily Lytton, the daughter of the former Viceroy of India. To satisfy the Lytton family, which was initially opposed to the match, Lutyens was obliged to take out an expensive life insurance policy, which exacerbated the financial worries which affected him all his life and which made him often over-anxious to obtain work. Although it produced five children, it was a difficult and often unhappy marriage. Estrangement was widened by Lady Emily first taking up Theosophy and then the cause of Indian independence, which did not assist her husband in his struggle to build New Delhi. They seemed to communicate best when apart, and the surviving correspondence between husband and wife maintained throughout the remainder of his life is a principal source for understanding his thoughts and ideas.

Following Munstead Wood, a creative essay in the Surrey vernacular, beautifully made, Lutyens designed a succession of romantic country houses – really *villas* – which established his reputation and which are among the principal glories of British architecture in that vital period around 1900. In them, he explored the possibilities of the tall brick chimney, the continuous roof plane and the timber-framed, leaded-light window, integrating house and garden through formal and material linear extensions and disciplining the vernacular language with an impeccable sense of form. That wise architect and critic H. S. Goodhart-Rendel once wrote of 'the sudden unanalysable felicity that makes one catch one's breath' in his work; as Lutyens himself put it, 'everything should have an air of inevitability', as it certainly did in his early houses as well as in his later, Classical work. After Lutyens's death, his great

American near-contemporary Frank Lloyd Wright was able to 'voice admiration of the love, loyalty and art with which this cultured architect, in love with Architecture, shaped his buildings. To him the English chimney, the Gable, the Gatepost monumentalized in good brickwork and cut-stone were motifs to be dramatized with great skill. He was able to idealize them with a success unequalled.' 'You cannot go far wrong in building-colour if you use local materials,' Lutyens once wrote. 'There is wit, and there may be humour, in the use of material.'

The names of Lutyens's early houses form a litany of romantic and rural aspiration in a rose-tinted view of Edwardian England: The Orchards, Fulbrook, Overstrand Hall, Tigbourne Court, Deanery Garden – for Edward Hudson, Goddards, Marsh Court ... Some were more eccentric, almost *Art Nouveau*, and comparable with the work of Charles Voysey or that of another now-famous contemporary, Charles Rennie Mackintosh. These more experimental houses included Berry Down, the Ferry Inn at Rosneath – for Queen Victoria's interesting wayward artistic daughter, HRH Princess Louise – and a remarkable house in France, Le Bois des Moutiers, but these are all less well known as they were regarded as not English or gentlemanly enough to be published in *Country Life*. In his exhaustive study of *Das englische Haus*, the Berlin architect Hermann Muthesius – who had been attached to the German embassy in London to study English domestic architecture, and learn from it – naturally noticed Lutyens and described him as 'a young man who of recent years has come increasingly to the forefront of domestic architects and who may soon become the accepted leader among English builders of houses, like Norman Shaw in the past. Lutyens is one of those architects who would refuse to have anything whatever to do with any new movement. His buildings reflect his attachment to the styles of the past, the charm of which he finds inexhaustible. [...] But just as a really important artist cannot ignore the demands of his time, so Lutyens's new buildings do not really look ancient at all. On the contrary, they have a character that, if not modern, is entirely personal and extremely interesting.'

Muthesius's book was first published in 1904, and if Lutyens had died that year rather than forty years later, he would still be remembered as the creator of some of the loveliest and most romantic houses ever built in England. But it was around this date that his work began to change direction. He was increasingly longing to tackle a 'big work' and was responding to the Edwardian interest in a more formal and disciplined architectural language, that is, the Classicism of Renaissance Italy. This taste for order, symmetry and grandeur was partly encouraged by the South African War, which generated a mood of defensive, even paranoid, imperialism and exaggerated patriotism in Britain. Even in the country house sphere, Arts and Crafts architects had come to recognise that the gentlemanly domestic tradition of Wren and the Georgian rectory was just as English, and as legitimate a model, as the timbered vernacular of earlier centuries. In consequence, Lutyens – who, like all his generation, uncritically revered Sir Christopher Wren – designed a number of restrained brick houses which can loosely be categorised as Neo-Georgian (and include some of his dullest creations). In 1903 he expressed his new enthusiasms in a letter to Herbert Baker, now in South Africa. 'In architecture Palladio is the game!! It is so big – few appreciate it now, and it requires training to value and realise it. The way Wren handled it was marvellous. Shaw has the gift. To the average man it is dry bones, but under the hand of a Wren it glows and the stiff material become as plastic clay. […] It is a game that never deceives, dodges never disguise. It means hard thought all through – if it is laboured it fails. […] So it is a big game, a high game […].'

Lutyens had, in fact, been playing this game almost from the beginning. Classical elements appeared in some of his early houses, like Overstrand Hall and Fulbrook, often deconstructed or artfully manipulated. His playing with the Classical language, what historians call Mannerism when referring to sixteenth-century Italy, is particularly evident in the impressively varied and original designs of his chimney-pieces, at which he was a master. Interestingly, Lutyens knew his Italian sources only from published photographs and he visited Italy for the first time as late as 1909 when invited to design the British Pavilion at the International Exhibition held in Rome that year (subsequently rebuilt as the British School at Rome). 'It is all very wonderful,' he wrote to his wife, 'and to see the things one knows from illustrations … Down a little street and then a corner and lo and behold stands some old loved friend in form of a doorway, staircase or palace. I recognise some of them by their backs – backs which I had never seen. […] There is so much here in little ways of things I thought I had invented! No wonder people think I must have been in Italy. Perhaps I have but it was not Rome.' Arrogant as this might seem, there is no doubt that Lutyens – without any formal training in the Classical orders – had an intuitive understanding of the expressive possibilities of the Classical language, of manipulation and abstraction.

9. '*Aedificavi, London*': the concept for St Quentin, realised at Thiepval, sketched on a sheet of Lutyens's office writing paper.

Lutyens's first large essay in what he called the 'Wrennaissance' was the new office building for *Country Life* in Covent Garden commissioned by Hudson in 1904, an essay on the theme of Hampton Court. But the building which many have seen as a turning point in Lutyens's work as marking a full acceptance of the Classical discipline was an unlikely expensive villa called Heathcote, at Ilkley in the West Riding of Yorkshire. Designed in 1906 for J. T. Hemingway, a Bradford wool exporter, Heathcote was inspired in its style by the Porta del Palio at Verona by Michele Sanmicheli. In this pretentious stone suburban house, Lutyens explored the possibilities of both rustication and the Roman Doric order, playing Mannerist games with both. It was here that he first used his favourite device − which later maddened Nikolaus Pevsner − of a pilaster which has a capital and a base but which disappears into the pattern of rusticated stones in between. Lutyens once remarked that 'Architecture is building with wit', and after his death H. S. Goodhart-Rendel observed that 'By his extraordinary accomplishment he brought the Classical orders completely under his control, a rare achievement in an Englishman, but his perpetual boyishness led him sometimes to play Classical pranks the humour of which may pall.'

In another letter to Baker written a few years later − often quoted as it is so revealing − Lutyens explained how he arrived at the design and how 'unconsciously the San Michele invention repeated itself. That time-worn Doric order − a lovely thing − I have the cheek to adopt. You can't copy it. To be right you have to take it and design it. You, as an exercise, take the order out of a book, as it stands, and couple the columns [...]. See what happens? Your bases interlock!

Inigo Jones solved the difficulty in one way and very good. Vanbrugh failed lamentably and clumsily. Wren avoided the problem. […] You cannot copy: you find if you do you are caught, a mess remains. It means hard labour, hard thinking, over every line in all three dimensions and in every joint; and no stone can be allowed to slide. If you tackle it in this way, the Order belongs to you, and every stroke, being mentally handled, must become endowed with such poetry and artistry as God has given you. You alter one feature (which you have to, always), then every other feature has to sympathise and undergo some care and invention. Therefore it is no mean [game], nor is it a game you can play lightheartedly.'

Such was the intellectual and mathematical rigour and sophisticated comprehension of three-dimensional form – of which Baker, like most other Edwardians, was incapable – with which Lutyens approached the handling of the Renaissance Classical language. He became increasingly interested in proportion, geometry and abstraction, as well as in the use of the optical corrections, or *entasis*, found on Greek temples like the Parthenon (which he did not actually visit until 1932). In his little book published in 1942, Robert Lutyens attempted an analysis of his father's compositions in terms of an 'armature of planes' and complex, standard proportional relationships which governed the angles of mouldings and roof planes ('which Father told me he could not understand a word of', his sister Mary later recalled). But Lutyens also knew that mathematics was a means to an end, that behind any system or style there needed to be subconscious or supernatural inspiration to achieve a great work of art.

Lutyens attempted to explain his understanding of creativity in a letter to his wife written in 1907. 'There is that in art which transcends all rules, it is the divine – I use poor words – and this is what makes all the arts so absorbing and thrilling to follow, creating a furore. […] There is the same effect produced on all and in all work by a master mind. To short sight it is a miracle, to those a little longer sighted it is Godhead, if we could see yet better, these facts may be revealed before which the V[ery] God as we conceive him will fade dim. It is the point of view that ought to bring all arts, Architecture, Sculpture, Painting, Literature and Music etc. into sympathy and there is no ploy which cannot be lifted to the divine level by its creation as an art.' In quoting this letter in his biography, Christopher Hussey observed how this 'is as near as he ever came to stating, in words, the belief which became his religion that perfect shapes and relationships – architectural facts arrived at empirically and by "refinement after refinement" – have in them a supra-natural, an eternal, relevance; are indeed reflections of divinity. It was this conviction that he at last sought to embody in his elemental designs' – not least in the Memorial to the Missing of the Somme.

At first, Lutyens was given few opportunities to play his high game in a big work. He was bitterly disappointed by his failure to win the competition for the County Hall of the London County Council in 1908 and only had consolation in the commission for twin churches in the centre of Hampstead Garden Suburb and in his design for the Theosophical Society's headquarters in Bloomsbury (now the British Medical Association) thanks to his wife's embracing this new religion and her friendship with Annie Besant. The real opportunities came abroad, first in South Africa with the Johannesburg Art Gallery, and then with the commission most architects could only dream of: for a great government building in the centre of a new planned city, New Delhi. The transfer of the capital of British India from Calcutta to Delhi was announced in 1911 and Lutyens was asked to join the Delhi Planning Commission the following year. Somehow, despite the vacillations of the Viceroy and the machinations of other jealous architects, he managed to wangle the job of designing the new city and the building which would dominate it: the great domed palace which would eventually be called Viceroy's House. In 1913, recognising he could not handle all the work himself, he suggested that his old friend Herbert Baker be brought in to design the flanking Secretariat buildings. It was a collaboration that would end in tears.

Viceroy's House – now Rashtrapati Bhavan – is one of the great buildings of the world. In it, Lutyens achieved a synthesis of East and West, fusing into the essentially Western, Classical composition Indian features such as the *chujja* – the projecting Moghul cornice – and wrapped elements from the Buddhist Great Stupa at Sanchi around his imperious dome. But it was no conventional Classical composition, relying on the pedantic expression of the orders; rather it is a powerful, dynamic composition of massive thick walls organised as a series of horizontal layers which, at lower levels, are projected to form retaining walls. In his eulogy of Lutyens's achievement when it was finally completed in 1931, Robert Byron wrote of this 'dynamic quality' and the use of a 'faintly pyramidal principle' in the design. 'Our age,' he argued, 'despite its physical enslavement by the machine and the mass, has discovered that joy in the sensuous beauty of the world perpetuated by the works of the Italian Renascence. The Viceroy's House at New Delhi is the first real justification of a new architecture which has already produced much that is worthy, but, till now, nothing of the greatest.'

Viceroy's House, placed at the focus of axial vistas, may be compared in its grandeur and intention to Versailles, or the Capitol in Washington, DC, although in architectural quality it transcends both. As the American historian Henry-Russell Hitchcock observed, 'Towards the designing of such a major monument generations of Frenchmen and others who had studied at the Beaux-Arts had been prepared; there is a certain irony that the opportunity came to an Englishman, trained in the most private and individualistic English way.' But comparisons with the work of Mansart, or even Wren, are ultimately not helpful. The design of Viceroy's House was in a tradition, but it was also unprecedented – modern – in both its massing and in such aspects as having columns of different heights rising to the same continuous entablature. Lutyens seems to have believed that in his conception he was expressing eternal absolutes. Resisting the pressure to adopt the Moghul arch – as used in the contemporary Indo-Saracenic style – to achieve a political compromise by mollifying those who felt that the new city should not be European in character, he argued that 'One cannot tinker with the round arch. God did not make the Eastern rainbow pointed to show his wide sympathies.'

Work had hardly begun on New Delhi when war broke out in August 1914. This was calamitous for most architects, as work dried up and commissions were cancelled. Twelve of Lutyens's assistants volunteered for service and the main office in Queen Anne's Gate was closed and moved to the New Delhi office in Apple Tree Yard. Lutyens was fortunate, however; not only was he invited to (neutral) Spain to build but work on the new capital continued until 1917. The regular winter visits to India continued; on his last wartime trip out, in November 1916, the ship was pursued and attacked by two German submarines after leaving Marseilles. Although there is no reason to suppose that his reaction to the war was anything other than conventional (among those back home), he was at first rather selfishly detached from it both because he was preoccupied with the unhappiness of his marriage and also because he was busy fighting his own battles with Baker and the government over the design of New Delhi. Too late, he had discovered that, by raising up the Secretariat buildings to the same level as Viceroy's House on Raisina Hill, the gradient between them on the central axial vista blocked the view of his portico from a distance. For practical reasons, Baker had compromised with expediency rather than remain firm to artistic principles – to Lutyens's disgust. The argument was taken to the highest level, the King, but it was no good: as Lutyens remarked, in one of his best puns, he had met his Bakerloo.

Lutyens was knighted in 1918. He was now much in demand and the jobs flowed in (although he continued to worry about money until the end). Further fame came when he devoted a great deal of time and effort to that curious piece of patriotic whimsy Queen Mary's Dolls' House – 'one of the few really dull things Lutyens has done', as John Summerson rightly observed. In the 1920s he was often invited to act as consulting architect on commercial projects in London designed by others (some of which brought him little credit). In Finsbury Circus he raised a multi-storey Palladian palace into the sky for Anglo-Persian Oil. Thanks to his friendship with Reginald McKenna, he designed facades for several buildings erected by the Midland Bank, notably the headquarters in Poultry in the City of London, where the proportional relationships and optical corrections on the extraordinary facade were calculated to small fractions of an inch. In Fleet Street he designed the building for Reuters. For Westminster City Council he designed blocks of public housing in Page Street which were enlivened by an abstract chequer-board pattern on the flat facades. And then there were more war memorials, in Southampton, Leicester, Rochdale and elsewhere.

There were a few big houses, notably Gledstone Hall in Yorkshire in which Lutyens reworked Palladian themes. One of his last jobs, carried out with his son Robert, was the rebuilding of Middleton Park in Oxfordshire for the Earl of Jersey and his wife, the American actress Virginia Cherrill, the former Mrs Cary Grant. Not all this late work was Classical, for Lutyens never forgot his roots and early enthusiasms. For his old friend Edward Hudson he enlarged Plumpton Place in Sussex using oak, plaster and tile, and at Cockington in Devon he built the Drum Inn in a modern vernacular, with a thatched roof. 'I enjoy all construction, and the steel girder with its petticoat of concrete is a most useful ally in the ever recurring advent of difficulty,' he wrote in 1932. 'But I crave for soft thick noiseless walls of hand-made brick and lime, the deep light reflecting reveals, the double floors, easy stairways, and doorways never less than 1 ft. 6 ins. from a corner. The waste of space, which unwittingly creates that most valuable asset, a gain of space.' Although he had sympathy and understanding for the enthusiasms of the young, he could never be reconciled to the austere utilitarianism and mechanistic styling of the Modern Movement. 'Architecture, with its love and passion, begins where function ends' was his motto. In reviewing the English translation of Le Corbusier's *Towards a New Architecture* in 1928, Lutyens noted that 'The Parthenon cost three times, and the gold and ivory statue of Athene seven times, the National Revenue. How is it possible to compare such a building with an aeroplane, which one faulty stay or bolt may crash to the ground?'

Above all, there was the great cathedral to be built for the Roman Catholics of Liverpool. It was commissioned in 1929 and in 1934 a magnificent timber model of Lutyens's conception – to be bigger than St Peter's in Rome – was exhibited at the Royal Academy. Twenty years earlier, he had written to Baker that 'You may laugh at me a bit, but *au fond* somewhere, I am horribly religious, but cannot speak it, and this saves my work.' The governing idea for the interior was the hierarchy of arches along two axes that was realised at Thiepval, except that here the nave and aisles were to be three times as high as their width – giving an almost Gothic proportion – rather than two and a half times. In the event, only part of the crypt had been built when the outbreak of another war in 1939 put paid to this most ambitious project. Even so, as Summerson later wrote, 'It will survive as an architectural creation of the highest order, perhaps as the latest and supreme attempt to embrace Rome, Byzantium, the Romanesque and the Renaissance in one triumphal and triumphant synthesis.' And, as far as Lutyens's son Robert was concerned, 'It could and should have been built. It may well have been the final affirmation of his faith in the eternal thing that so transcends mere building. It is architecture – asserted once and for ever – and the very greatest building that was never built!'

The truth of these hyperbolic assertions – made by men who knew what they were talking about – can at least be grasped at Thiepval. And of all the designs actually realised by Lutyens after the Great War, the greatest were those undertaken for the Imperial War Graves Commission. The work meant much to him; as he had written from Boulogne to a client in 1925, 'I am here doing Graves in France, and the magnitude of that host of boys that lie fearfully still, quickens the senses of unspeakable desolation.'

Back in June 1917, Lutyens had been surprised and honoured to be invited by the newly established Imperial War Graves Commission to advise on the treatment of the proposed military cemeteries; according to his new friend Lady Sackville, he was 'very emotional' about this. The following month he was invited – along with the Director of the Tate Gallery and the wretched, ubiquitous Baker – to visit the battlefields in France to study the problems involved and see the temporary, makeshift cemeteries. They were billeted in a *château* near Montreuil and, naturally, were not allowed near the fighting (even so, perhaps they saw quite as much of the conditions at the front line as some high-ranking officers). It is therefore quite possible the cemeteries they saw were those in the old Somme battlefield area. From France, Lutyens sent a much-quoted letter which described the shocking things he saw and is profoundly revealing about his attitude both to the war and to architecture.

'The cemeteries, the dotted graves, are the most pathetic thing,' he wrote to his wife, 'specially when one thinks of how things are run and problems treated at home. What humanity can endure and suffer is beyond belief. The battlefields – the obliteration of all human endeavour and achievement and the human achievement of destruction is bettered by the poppies and wild flowers that are as friendly to an unexploded shell as

10. The great arch at Thiepval …

11. ... a theme which was developed in Lutyens's unexecuted design for the Metropolitan Cathedral in Liverpool, seen here in an interior perspective sketch by the architect in 1933.

they are to the leg of a garden seat in Surrey. It is all a sense of wonderment, how can such things be. […] One is seeing very little of all there is to be seen but the little is ominous of what lies beyond a battlefield, with the blessed trenches, the position of a machine gun by its litter of spent cartridges. The ruined tanks, the rough broken shell-hole pitted ground, you assume was once a village. A small bit of wall of what was once a church may stand but nothing else. The half ruined places are more impressive for there you can picture what a place might have been. The graveyards, haphazard from the needs of much to do and little time for thought. And then a ribbon of isolated graves like a milky way across miles of country where men were tucked in where they fell. Ribbons of little crosses each touching each across a cemetery, set in a wilderness of annuals and where one sort of flower is grown the effect is charming, easy and oh so pathetic. One thinks for the moment no other monument is needed. Evanescent but for the moment is almost perfect and how misleading to surmise in this emotion and how some love to sermonise. But the only monument can be one where the endeavour is sincere to make such monument permanent – a solid ball of bronze!'

That concept of a solid ball of bronze, or a pure monument relying on abstract geometry – so interestingly reminiscent of Boullée's projects – would soon be transformed into the idea of the Great War Stone, a subtly modelled monolith which would be placed in every cemetery. It was at this moment, in that most dreadful year 1917, that Lutyens's belief in an elemental, timeless architecture which had resonance through tradition coincided with a terrible purpose, and the War Graves Commission and its founder, Fabian Ware, had the wit to see that this concept was appropriate. Resisting the strong, emotional demand – not least from Baker – to employ the cross and other more literal symbolic forms, they adopted a severely secular language to commemorate the dead in a war that did not distinguish between victims by either race or religion. Exasperated and alienated as he was by Lady Emily's own absorption with Theosophy, Lutyens was sympathetic to its pantheism and to its belief in the fundamental unity of all faiths. His tolerance, combined with a belief in the power and appropriateness of pure architecture, had a profound influence on the humane attitude of the War Graves Commission to its task and on the quality of its achievement.

....

4

THE WAR GRAVES COMMISSION

The Imperial War Graves Commission was essentially the creation of one remarkable man, Sir Fabian Ware (1869–1949). An exact contemporary of Lutyens, Ware had been a teacher, an educational reformer and, as assistant director of education for the Transvaal, a member of Lord Milner's 'kindergarten' of administrators in South Africa as well as editor of the *Morning Post*. Ware certainly belonged to that generation of cultivated bullies who ran the Edwardian Empire with supreme confidence, but he was not typical; he was a man with a strong social conscience and wide sympathies as well as being possessed of remarkable energy. On the outbreak of war, Ware offered his services to the Red Cross and soon found himself organising a 'flying unit' of private cars and drivers assisting the French army. In the course of assisting the wounded during the confused campaigns of 1914, Ware became more and more concerned with locating and recording the graves of the dead – something of little concern to the military authorities at first. He pointed out that no one had the responsibility of recording and maintaining the growing number of war graves. With the support of General Sir Nevil Macready, Adjutant-General to the British Expeditionary Force, who was mindful of the distress caused by the neglect of graves during the Boer War, the War Office officially recognised Ware's Graves Registration Commission in March 1915.

Ware pointed out that although his Commission's work had no military importance, it had 'an extraordinary moral value to the troops in the field as well as to the relatives and friends of the dead at home' and that when hostilities were eventually terminated, the government would have to do something about the thousands and thousands of graves, many scattered over the battlefields, some dug in French churchyards. The poet Edmund Blunden, who had fought on the Somme and who succeeded Kipling as the Commission's unofficial literary adviser, later recalled that 'not many soldiers retained the confidence that the dead – themselves, it might be, to-morrow or the next instant – would at length obtain some lasting and distant memorial. [...] The assemblies of wooden crosses in the wrecked villages near the line, with here and there an additional sign of remembrance suggested by the feeling and opportunity of fellow-soldiers, seemed to have a poor chance of remaining recognisable or visible after one more outburst of attack or counterblast, when high explosive or torrential steel would tear up the soil over deliberately chosen spaces of the land.'

Ware badgered the authorities to ensure that graves were recorded and, if possible, maintained; he also commenced negotiations with the French to establish the status of the war cemeteries in the future. Ware realised that the task of creating proper graves and cemeteries would be immense, and that it would concern all the constituent parts of the British Empire. He also was concerned that proper policies be established for war graves, and that rich families were not able to erect more elaborate memorials or take bodies back to Britain for burial. Ware knew that 'in ninety-nine cases out of a hundred' officers 'will tell you that if they are killed [they] would wish to be among their men' and he made sure that exhumations were forbidden. As Philip Longworth, historian of the War Graves Commission, has written, Ware 'sensed the new and democratic mood which was taking hold of the Army. Traditional though he was in many ways, he had read Bergson, Rousseau, Marx and the Syndicalists and had been influenced by some of their ideas.' Ware was a complex figure; although a 'social imperialist' and the former editor of a right-wing newspaper, he was sympathetic towards the Labour movement and anxious for social reform. The Imperial War Graves Commission, as it was established by Royal Charter in April 1917, would achieve equality for all the dead – whether rich or poor, officers or private soldiers, titled or common.

This task was something quite new. No such concern for the treatment of the dead had been demonstrated by the authorities in earlier conflicts. After the Battle of Waterloo, for instance – the bloodiest battle for the British before 1914, in which the casualties were some 5,100 dead out of a total of 50,000 dead and wounded on both sides – while the bodies of officers were mostly taken home for burial those of private soldiers were dumped in mass graves. Only in 1889, by order of Queen Victoria, were the dead of Waterloo belatedly honoured at the Evere Cemetery in Brussels when the bodies of officers, non-commissioned officers and men were reinterred there (this was probably the first British national memorial to the dead, as opposed to a monument to a victory). The British government cared little more after the war with Russia in 1854–6, although a proper military cemetery was established,

12. A belated tribute: the monument and mausoleum erected in the Evere Cemetery in Brussels in 1889 by order of Queen Victoria for the bodies of British officers and men left on the field of Waterloo.

by necessity, at Scutari with graves for 8,000 who died of wounds and disease next to the hospital run by Florence Nightingale (later enhanced by a granite obelisk with angels carved by Baron Marochetti). As Ware stressed in his memorandum proposing an 'Imperial Commission for the Care of Soldiers' Graves' in 1917, the Empire must be 'spared the reflections which weighed on the conscience of the British nation when, nearly twenty years after the conclusion of the Crimean War, it became known that the last resting place of those who had fallen in that war had, except in individual instances, remained uncared for and neglected'.

It was after the American Civil War, the first modern war in that it was total and involved whole populations, with huge casualties occurring in conscripted armies, that proper official cemeteries were established for all ranks. An Act promoted by President Lincoln in 1862 allowed for the creation of fourteen national cemeteries for all the Union dead. A similar concern was manifested by both sides after the Franco-Prussian War. As wars became larger in scale, fought by conscripted soldiers rather than by professional armies (on which the British still relied until 1916), so the popular concern for the fate and last resting place of the individual soldier increased. In the Great War of 1914–18, parliamentary governments as well as autocracies committed their populations to the struggle with a ruthless subservience to the national cause inconceivable in earlier centuries ('Are we to continue until we have killed ALL our young men?' Lord Lansdowne, the former Foreign Secretary, asked the Cabinet at the end of the Battle of the Somme). The patriotic and nationalistic character of the war demanded that every individual sacrifice be commemorated, although the chaos and social breakdown that resulted in some of the fighting powers, Russia and Turkey above all, rendered this impossible.

The task faced by the newly established Imperial War Graves Commission, of giving decent burial and permanent commemoration to hundreds of thousands of casualties, was horribly exacerbated by the nature of the war. Blunden described how, on the Somme, 'men perished in great multitudes and in places where their bodies could not be recovered, so intense was the new artillery and machine-gun fire, so hopeless the mud which went on for miles. The battalions who came up to the relief of those in the craters and vestiges of trenches would find themselves, in the fire-splashed night, stumbling over corpse after corpse. In deep dug-outs, twenty or thirty feet down, friends or foes were done to death by one means or another with the ultimate result that there was no entering those burnt-out, dreadful caverns.' After the even greater horror of Passchendaele, when 'a deeper, fouler slime drowned all but the luckiest life in man and nature [...], the soldier felt that his death would be his complete and final disappearance. The Book of Life was for others. [...] At that period, the idea that these battlefields would themselves ever again become pasture-lands, and châteaux with grounds and little lakes and garden-walls, would have appeared sheer fantasy.'

As work on the cemeteries could not proceed until after the end of hostilities, Ware first established principles to govern the Commission's approach and sought expert advice – hence the visit by Lutyens and Baker to France in July 1917. To a remarkable extent, the recommendations made by Lutyens in a Memorandum written the following month were adopted as official policy. In particular, there was his suggestion of an identical abstract monumental form in all the proposed cemeteries: 'I most earnestly advise that there shall be one kind of monument throughout, whether in Europe, Asia or Africa, and that it shall take the form of one great fair stone of fine proportions, twelve feet in length, lying raised upon three steps, of which the first and third shall be twice the width of the second; and that each stone shall bear in indelible lettering, some fine thought or words of sacred dedication. They should be known in all places and for all time, as the Great War Stones, and should stand, though in three Continents, as equal monuments of devotion, suggesting the thought of memorial Chapels in one vast Cathedral.' (J. M. Barrie had suggested calling it a *stone* rather than an *altar* as, knowing the Presbyterian prejudices of his countrymen, 'The Scotch [...] wouldn't like the word.')

Such was the transformation of Lutyens's aspiration for 'a solid ball of bronze' into the concept of what became known as the Stone of Remembrance although, in fact, he had already described the stone idea to Ware in a letter written in May 1917 – before he went to see the battlefields. In this, he recommended that the 'great stone of fine proportion twelve feet long set fair or finely wrot – without undue ornament and tricky and elaborate carvings and inscribe thereon one thought in clear letters so that all men for all time may read and know the reasons why these stones are so placed throughout France – facing the West and facing the men who lie looking ever eastward towards the enemy – after this you can plant to desire and erect cloisters – chapels – crosses buildings of as many varieties as to suit the always varying sites'. In the event, these monoliths on their shallow steps – bearing the inscription from the *Book of Ecclesiasticus* 'THEIR NAME

LIVETH FOR EVERMORE', chosen by Kipling, and carefully modelled and enlivened with *entasis*: curves that were part of a hypothetical sphere exactly 1,801 feet 8 inches in diameter – were placed in all the Commission's cemeteries apart from the very smallest.

Jane Ridley points out that the spherical surface on stone and steps was a symbol of hope and that 'For Lutyens the symbol of happiness had always been a circle.' The very idea of the Great War Stone was a faintly pagan concept and thus provoked opposition from those who wanted conventional Christian symbolism in the cemeteries and, later, on the Cenotaph. The other two who visited France with Lutyens, Baker and Aitken, both recommended a cross for each cemetery; Baker, indeed, with his love of literal symbolism, even suggested a cross with five points, one for each colony. Lutyens wrote to his wife about this last silly idea and that 'India, Ware pointed out, was forgotten, but what does a five pointed cross mean? Ware bids me courage.' And Lady Emily responded that 'Baker must be dotty! A five pointed cross for each of the colonies. Too silly. And India left out which will cause bitter hurt and what about the Jews and agnostics who hate crosses?'

For all his racial prejudice engendered by both convention and by Emily's obsession with Krishnamurti as the new World Teacher, Lutyens was at one with his wife in his pantheistic and non-sectarian conception of religion and culture. Fortunately Fabian Ware, whom Lutyens immediately admired and got on very well with, agreed. ('Mon General,' Lutyens's letters to him often began, and he sometimes signed himself 'Votre Toujours Subaltern'; Ware, like others who worked for the Commission, took military rank, but although

[79]

13. Lutyens's Great War Stone or Stone of Remembrance, placed in the centre of his Memorial at Thiepval.

Lutyens was asked to be a captain he declined: 'I could not go about in khaki with straps of a sword I cannot and could not use etc.!') Lutyens wrote to Ware in August 1917 about the war stone: 'Labour members, Jews, R. Catholics, Non-conformists, ladies of fashion especially those that suffer a loss, all seem to like it and agree in the banality of the †:, I have not had the courage to tackle a Bishop, but do you think it wise if I asked Cantuar to see me, he would I think, but if I catch sight of the apron it is apt, at a critical moment, to give me the giggles, especially when they get pompous and hold their hands across their knees – why?' Lutyens seemed not to have cared much for the established Church and was certainly concerned not to cause offence to other religions. There is no evidence to suggest, however, that he disliked the way that the Christian churches had identified God's will so closely with the national cause (in every nation). He might well have done; as one serving officer recorded, 'the Christian Churches are the finest blood-lust creators which we have and of them we made free use'.

In the event, Lutyens did show his war stone proposal to Randall Davidson, Archbishop of Canterbury, who at first indicated approval but later wrote to Ware to condemn it and to demand a cross. Lutyens recorded that Ware 'was "shocked, grieved" at the Archbishop's letter – expected a neutral attitude not a narrow antagonistic view. He says the clergy in France are most tiresome – always trying to upset any and every kind of applecart. But he thinks the "stone" will win yet [...].' It did, but in view of the strength of the demand for Christian imagery in the war cemeteries, a compromise was eventually established. In addition to the Stone of Remembrance, every cemetery would also contain a free-standing cross. But how pleased Lutyens must have been when he was able to write to the Archbishop in 1923 that 'I was so glad to see in today's paper that the Great War Stone in a cemetery was used as an Altar for the administration of Holy Communion.'

The Cross of Sacrifice, found in many places in Britain as well as in every war cemetery, was designed by Reginald Blomfield and consists of an octagonal stepped base supporting a tall stone cross on which is fixed a bronze sword. This, although handsome, gives the cemeteries a touch of precisely that 'Onward, Christian Soldiers!' tone that Ware and Lutyens strove to avoid (Lutyens also designed a cross, faceted and compact, and with no sword, that can sometimes be found in churchyards and used as a war memorial in England). The problems sometimes created by this Christian symbolism are suggested by Lutyens's comments on the official report approving the design for Choques Military Cemetery in 1920 in which he apologised to the Assistant Architect as 'I did not realise the cross came so close to the Jewish plot & it would be good manners to move it to a central position south.' (In defence both of the Church and of the French, it is worth noting that Ware paid tribute to Mgr Julien, Bishop of Arras, who never ceased to remind his compatriots that 'in the sight of God the dead of Germany were the equals of the dead of France'.)

Equally controversial was the question of the design of the permanent gravestones and whether they should be uniform. As already mentioned, Ware had made sure that private exhumations for reburial back home were banned (a policy that was unique to Britain) and he was determined that this prohibition was maintained and that private monuments were

14. The standard Cross of Sacrifice designed by Sir Reginald Blomfield in the Military Cemetery at Villers-Bretonneux; in the background is Lutyens's Australian National War Memorial with its lookout tower.

not to be permitted in the war cemeteries. The Commission announced in January 1918 that 'it would be inadvisable to leave the provision of memorials to private initiative. If memorials were allowed to be erected in the War Cemeteries according to the preference, taste and means of relatives and friends, the result would be that costly monuments put up by the well-to-do over their dead would contrast unkindly with those humbler ones which would be all that poor folk could afford. Thus the inspiring memory of the common sacrifice made by all ranks would lose the regularity and orderliness most becoming to the resting places of soldiers, who fought and fell side by side [...].' This crucial principle of equality of treatment, that there was to be no distinction between the graves of officers and men, was fully endorsed by Lutyens, who, in his Memorandum, recommended that 'every grave will be marked with a headstone bearing the soldier's name and rank, and possibly the sculptured badge of his regiment, also some symbol denoting his religious faith. [...] All that is done of structure should be for endurance for all time and for equality of honour, for besides Christians of all denominations, there will be Jews, Mussulmens, Hindus and men of other creeds; their glorious names and their mortal bodies all equally deserving enduring record and seemly sepulture.'

Lutyens revealed more of his feelings about this in a letter to his wife in which he argued 'That the most beautiful sites should be selected not where the victories were and all that snobbery, for I hold that there is equality in sacrifice and the men who fell at Quatre Bras are just as worthy of honour as those that fell at Waterloo. I do not want to put worldly value over our dead. They put "killed in action" or "died from wounds", "died". Died alone means some defalcation and shot for it. I don't like it. The mother lost her boy and it was in the interests of the country and she had to suffer – her boy. Do you see what I mean? But then I don't fight nor do I fight yet for the seemly sepulture of the Germans when they lie along with our men.' Emily did see what he meant. 'I am very keen about your stone,' she replied. 'It appeals to *my* side of life – as houses don't and I see much true symbolism in it. [...] I am also entirely at one with you about equality of sacrifice and that all those who "die" no matter from what cause should be honoured. I think it too awful that the wife of a man shot for cowardice gets no pension. After all he is equally lost to her and by government orders. I think it is barbarous.'

The Commission decided to adopt a standard secular headstone as Lutyens, and others, recommended. Of Portland stone with a curved top and straight sides, each bears the name of the man beneath in a fine Roman alphabet designed by Macdonald Gill, the brother of Eric Gill. A regimental badge and a religious symbol – a cross, or Star of David – could also be carved into the stone, together with a text if the soldier's family so requested. Over those many thousands of graves containing an unidentified body, the same headstone bears the poignant inscription – chosen by Kipling – 'A Soldier of the Great War / Known unto God.' As the Commission insisted, 'in death, all, from General to Private, of whatever race or creed, should receive equal honour under a memorial which should be the common symbol of their comradeship and of the cause for which they died'. The humanity and rightness of this decision is reinforced by comparison with the French war cemeteries, in which it can be painful to see a line of crosses broken by a gravestone in the shape of a Star of David or one given the profile of an Islamic arch.

15. Corbie Communal Cemetery Extension near the river Somme, designed by Charles Holden for the Imperial War Graves Commission, with lines of the standard British secular headstones.

With the war over, however, the policy of equality of treatment provoked growing opposition. Campaigns were mounted against the War Graves Commission which emphasised the cruelty of preventing families and bereaved relatives from having any say in the way soldiers were buried. Lady Florence Cecil, the wife of the Bishop of Exeter, who had lost three sons in the war, made a direct appeal 'in the name of thousands of heartbroken parents, wives, brothers and sisters' to the Prince of Wales as President of the Commission to permit a cross as an alternative to the standard headstone. 'It is only through the hope of the cross,' she wrote, 'that most of us are able to carry on the life from which all the sunshine seems to have gone, and to deny us the emblem of that strength and hope adds heavily to the burden of our sorrow.' Ultimately the matter was settled by Parliament and in a crucial and emotional debate on 4th May 1920 the Commission's policies were upheld. Equality in death, like equality in life, had to be enforced by the state, and the British people had to learn that liberty is incompatible with war, and that once a man had enlisted, his body – whether alive or dead – belonged to the King. It is nevertheless remarkable that such rigid egalitarianism and secularism was enforced by a parliamentary democracy so often characterised by compromise and by sentimental gestures.

Other general principles regarding the design of the cemeteries were less contentious. From the beginning, the importance of horticulture was stressed. The war cemeteries were intended to convey something of the character of the England the dead had fought for, an ideal England full of gardens and beautiful landscapes. Just as the Commission's work manifested the contemporary interest in Classical architecture, so it reflected the enthusiasm for garden design which flourished in the Edwardian years. The war cemeteries can almost be seen as a re-creation of that fusion of architecture and gardening, and that reconciliation of the formal and the picturesque approaches to garden design, achieved by the collaboration of Lutyens and his mentor, Gertrude Jekyll, before the war. Lutyens had recommended to the Commission that 'The design of any further arrangements, or of any planting of evergreen trees – Ilex, Box, Bay, Cypress, Yews or Juniper, or of other trees or shrubs of such a kind as may be suitable to a special climate, would be determined by the character of the buildings, and by the area and nature of the ground; but all should be planned on broad and simple lines [...]. But though it will be important to secure the qualities of repose and dignity there is no need for the cemeteries to be gloomy or even sad looking places. Good use should be made of the best and most beautiful flowering plants and shrubs [...].' Baker, for once, agreed, later writing that the cemeteries 'should express the sense of reverence and peace. [...] My own thoughts always turned to the beauty associated with churchyard and cloister, a sacred *place*, a *temenos*.'

Gertrude Jekyll prepared planting plans for four cemeteries for which Lutyens had responsibility – Hersin, Gézaincourt, Daours and La Neuville – as well as for Warlincourt Halte, which was designed by Holden. Jane Brown has argued that these set the pattern for all the others and that, under Lutyens's influence, the British war cemetery became 'the modern apotheosis of the secret garden [...] there is the enclosing evergreen (holly or yew) hedge, the symbolic fastigiated oak or Lombardy poplars, massings of workaday shrubs of the English countryside – blackthorn, whitethorn, hazel, guilder rose and honeysuckle – with the Virgin's flowering meads ushered into soft borders where the headstones stand, hellebores, narcissus, forget-me-not, fritillaries, foxgloves, columbines, London Pride, bergenia, nepeta and roses. These are Arts and Crafts gardens, outdoor rooms of green walls, their vistas ordered and closed by the most sublime stone works, most with book-room pavilions and shelters, all of them laced and imbued with meaning and double-meaning [...].' 'Those who doubt the power of landscape to console,' Ken Worpole has written, 'should visit some of these cemeteries, the design and care of which successfully embody and integrate so many nuances of public and private emotion.'

The Commission's architects were also generally agreed that for both the memorials and the shelter buildings required in each cemetery, monumental Classical architecture was enough and that little sculpture was needed. As Blomfield later recalled, 'many of us had seen terrible examples of war memorials in France and were haunted by the fear of winged angels in various sentimental attitudes'. Of the Commission's principal architects, Lutyens and Holden used the least sculpture and carving, Baker the most. Fine work was done for the Commission by Gilbert Ledward, Charles Wheeler, William Reid Dick, Ernest Gillick, Walter Gilbert, Laurence Turner and Charles Sergeant Jagger. Arguably the greatest British sculptor of the last century, Jagger was responsible for carved panels on the Memorial to the Missing at Louverval as well as for the reliefs and the bronze figures on his great masterpiece, the Artillery Memorial at Hyde Park Corner in London, in which the heroism and brutality of war is conveyed without any sentimentality.

Because of the disagreements between the architects first

consulted and about the methods to be used to secure designs, Sir Frederic Kenyon, Director of the British Museum, was invited to act as Architectural Adviser in November 1917 and he recommended the senior architects to be employed by the Commission. Lutyens, Baker and Blomfield were appointed Principal Architects for France and Belgium in March 1918. They were joined in 1920 by Charles Holden, who had already served as an Assistant Architect to the Commission and who applied his severe Neo-Classical style both to the war cemeteries and to the contemporary stations for the London Underground. Their salary was initially £400 per annum, raised to £600 in 1919. The Commission's work was not, however, confined to the Western Front. Sir Robert Lorimer, designer of the Scottish National War Memorial, was appointed Principal Architect for Italy, Macedonia and Egypt, and was responsible for rugged war cemeteries high up in the foothills of the Alps. Another Scot, the great Beaux-Arts-trained Glaswegian Sir John James Burnet, was appointed Principal Architect for Palestine and Gallipoli, and was assisted in his work by his partner Thomas Tait. Finally there was E. P. Warren, who was appointed Principal Architect for Mesopotamia and designed the Memorial to the Missing in Basra.

The task of designing and supervising the execution of hundreds of cemeteries in France and Belgium could not be undertaken by the Principal Architects alone, especially as all were also running their own private practices. On Kenyon's recommendation, the actual work of designing the many cemeteries was entrusted to younger architects who had served in the war, but supervised by the senior architects. This team of Assistant Architects was based at St Omer in France. One was South African – Gordon Leith – while Wilfrid Von

Berg, born in Croydon, would emigrate to South Africa; two were older, and had served in the London Ambulance Brigade of the Red Cross: Holden and W. H. Cowlishaw; the others were W. B. Binnie, G. H. Goldsmith (who had been Lutyens's assistant before the war), Frank Higginson, A. J. S. Hutton, Noël Rew and J. R. Truelove. In theory, the Principal Architect would make suggestions for a particular cemetery, and later approve or amend a sketch design made by the Assistant Architect. For the smallest cemeteries, with under 250 burials, the Assistant Architects would seem to have enjoyed more or less complete independence. 'In retrospect,' Ware later wrote, 'the chief merit of this system is seen to have been the variety of treatment which resulted from the free play thus given to the interest in individual cemeteries natural to architects who were dealing with burial places of their comrades in arms.'

The ultimate authorship of a particular war cemetery is often confirmed by the Commission's standard report sheets, on which the Principal Architect as well as the Horticultural Expert and the Deputy Director of Works would indicate approval or make suggestions. On that for the Chinese Labour Corps Cemetery at Noyelles-sur-Mer, which was designed by Truelove in an appropriate style, Lutyens wrote that 'I know nothing of Chinese art. I can but express my admiration. Capt Truelove should go to London and visit the British Museum and the wholesale Chinese warehouses in London.' It is clear from the cemeteries themselves that the principal influence on their architecture was that of Lutyens, although Lutyens himself may well have been influenced by the severely abstract work of Holden. At the end of his life, Von Berg wrote that 'Blomfield, I recall, took a meagre and superficial interest in my work and rarely had much to contribute. Lutyens, on the other hand, showed a lively concern coupled with a delicious sense of humour. I remember how once he introduced an asymmetrical feature into one of my designs saying with a chuckle "That's cockeye but let's do it" [...] Holden, serious and painstaking, was a senior architect for whom I had the greatest respect.'

The colossal task of caring for 580,000 identified and 180,000 unidentified graves was begun early in 1919. Some were in small temporary cemeteries, others scattered and isolated, so that bodies had to be moved to the permanent cemeteries to be constructed by the Commission. Today, when film makers wish to emphasise the carnage of the Great War, the camera often pans over a vast sea of crosses. But this, at least for British war cemeteries, gives a quite false impression. Not only are the British dead marked by standard headstones rather than crosses, but few of the cemeteries are very large and in most there are but several hundred headstones. Only in those sited near base-camps or hospitals where men died of their wounds, like Etaples and Lijssenthoek, are the graves to be counted in thousands. What is awe-inspiring – terrifying – about the British cemeteries of the Great War is not their size but their number. Even after the bodies in several hundred cemeteries had been moved, there were almost a thousand separate British war cemeteries constructed along the line of the Western Front between the North Sea and the Somme. Their very locations tell the story of the war. As John Keegan has written about the Battle of the Somme, along the old front line north of Thiepval, 'at intervals of a few hundred yards, run a line of the Commonwealth War Graves Commission's beautiful garden cemeteries, ablaze near the anniversary of the battle with rose and wisteria blossom, the white Portland stone of headstones and memorial crosses gleaming in the sun. […] A few […] stand a little forward of the rest, and mark the furthest limit of advance. The majority stand on the front line or in no man's land just outside the German wire. The soldiers who died there were buried where they had fallen. Thus the cemeteries are a map of the battle. The map tells a simple and terrible story.'

Because of the controversy over the Commission's policies, three experimental cemeteries were completed by 1920 to demonstrate what was being aimed at. It was first intended that each should be designed by one of the three Principal Architects but, in the event, the three – at Le Tréport, Louvencourt and Forceville – had Blomfield as Principal Architect. There is evidence, however, that Forceville, the most successful of these cemeteries, as well as Louvencourt, were actually the work of Holden as Blomfield's assistant and the economical severity of its design would serve as a model for the Commission's architects. These cemeteries were well received by the visiting British public; a correspondent for *The Times* considered that Forceville Communal Cemetery Extension, planted with yew hedges and lindens as well as flowers, was 'The most perfect, the noblest, the most classically beautiful memorial that any loving heart or any proud nation could desire to their heroes fallen in a foreign land.'

Lutyens, as Principal Architect, was responsible for designing or supervising 127 war cemeteries in France and Belgium, although many of these were actually the work of his former assistant, Goldsmith. Lutyens himself was certainly personally responsible for some of the larger cemeteries, notably Etaples Military Cemetery near Le Touquet, next to the site of the notorious 'Eat Apples' base camp – where a mutiny had occurred in 1917. Here, above stone retaining walls on rising land overlooking the railway from the Channel ports to Paris, he placed two extraordinary cenotaphs either side of the Stone of Remembrance. Each of these pylons rises above an arched base and is flanked by stone flags that hang ever still – as he wanted to do with the flags on the Cenotaph in London but was overruled. The design of a cemetery was scarcely a new problem, but Lutyens demonstrated here that he was able to rise to new heights of originality in abstracting and developing the Classical language of architecture to give dignity to these 'silent cities of the dead'.

Another impressive cemetery by Lutyens is that at Villers-Bretonneux, where Lutyens placed two exquisite lodges like eighteenth-century garden pavilions at the roadside entrance. From here, the ground rises in a gentle convex slope, past the Cross of Sacrifice standing between lines of headstones, to reach a wall covered in names each side of a look-out tower. This is the Australian National War Memorial, for it was here that Australian troops checked Ludendorff's offensive towards Amiens in 1918. Originally the memorial was to have been the work of the Australian architect William Lucas, who had won a competition in 1925, but his design was disliked by Ware and by General Sir Talbot Hobbs, who had chosen the site for the memorial. When the project was suspended in 1930 for economic reasons, Hobbs approached Lutyens instead (not for the first time did he cheerfully supplant another architect). The memorial as built is one of Lutyens's last and most idiosyncratic executed works; in the flanking pavilions and the observation pavilion at the top of the tower he returned to themes that had exercised him early

16. The extraordinary pylons rising above Etaples Military Cemetery: arched
cenotaphs flanked by the stone flags, eternally still, that Lutyens wanted to
use on the Cenotaph in Whitehall.

in his career, deconstructing Classical forms and making them hang, as it were, in space. This memorial was dedicated in 1938, completing the Commission's task.

Ware was distressed that the various constituent parts of the Empire chose to erect their own memorials as it undermined his vision of Imperial co-operation and also led to anomalies and the duplication of the names of the Missing in certain cases, but his persuasiveness – for once – was in vain. The Union of South Africa naturally turned to Baker for its memorial at Delville Wood, where hellish fighting had taken place during the Somme offensive. Baker was also responsible for the Indian Memorial at Neuve-Chapelle, one of his happiest works in which the Moghul, Hindu and Buddhist elements used at New Delhi were combined in a beautiful circular enclosure. New Zealand chose to build several memorials to its missing in different cemeteries. That at Grévillers is by Lutyens; the one at Caterpillar Valley by Baker; and those in Belgium, at Polygon Wood and Messines, were designed by Holden in his severe Neo-Classical style. Canada, however, chose not to use one of the Commission's architects but commissioned the Canadian sculptor Walter S. Allward to design its memorial at Vimy Ridge. The result was an extraordinary Expressionist creation with tall towers that dissolve into sculptured figures.

It is instructive to compare the British war cemeteries with those of the other fighting powers. The French chose to concentrate their dead in large cemeteries, with the bones of the many unidentified casualties put into ossuaries, as at Douamont near Verdun, where a strange monumental streamlined structure with a tower, designed by Azéma, Hardy & Edrei and built in 1923–32, encloses a long barrel-vaulted chamber containing thousands upon thousands of bones. As already stated, the gravestone adopted by the French was the cross, usually made of concrete, with a stamped tin label attached bearing the name of the dead man. These can be seen at Thiepval, where, below Lutyens's monument, a cemetery was laid out with equal numbers of bodies of both French and British unknown soldiers discovered on the site to emphasise the Anglo-French aspect of the Somme offensive and of the memorial. On one side of a central vista leading to the Cross of Sacrifice lie 300 white headstones of the British graves, each with the inscription 'A Soldier of the Great War known unto God'. On the other are the 300 French graves, with lines of concrete crosses each bearing a small rectangle of stamped tin with the single, pathetic word '*Inconnu*'.

A characteristic example of French war memorial architecture is the national memorial and cemetery of Notre-Dame de Lorette, north of Arras, where a tall lantern tower, containing an ossuary, and a basilica rise above a vast sea of crosses. There are 40,000 bodies in this melancholy and desperate place, 24,000 of them in marked graves. The buildings were designed by Louis-Marie Cordonnier and his son Jacques Cordonnier, architects of the basilica at Lisieux, and built in 1921-7. Artistically they are puzzling, as although there is a slight Art Deco or modernistic quality about the tower, the Byzantinesque church might well have been designed decades earlier. Such architecture exhibits nothing of the discipline and monumentality of the British war cemeteries and memorials. It is as if France had been so devastated by the war that her architects were unable to rise to the terrible occasion. The torch of Classicism, once kept alight at the Ecole-des-Beaux-Arts in Paris, would seem to have been passed to American architects, so many of whom were educated there. Their monumental but rather pedantic Classical memorials are to be found in the American war cemeteries east of the Somme, establishing a ratio between the volume of masonry and the number of casualties far in excess of those of other nations.

The Italians adopted a quite different approach and their official memorials are huge and extraordinary although still not well known. The Commissariato Generale Onoranze Caduti in Guerra was founded in 1919 under the Ministry of War but little was done to honour Italy's large number of ill-used casualties until after 1927 under the Fascist government of Mussolini. The bones of the dead were mostly placed in ossuaries, vast structures which were as much landscaped monuments as buildings. Some were in difficult, almost inaccessible sites: the 'sacrario' at Monte Grappa was constructed almost 6,000 feet up in the Venetian Alps. Those at Asiago and Redipuglia were not inaugurated until 1938.

The Germans were not permitted to erect memorials in the places in France and Belgium where so many of their soldiers died. Many bodies were eventually taken back to Germany; most were exhumed to be concentrated in a few cemeteries, often in mass graves. Where permanent cemeteries were constructed, with lodges and walls, they were designed in a rugged Arts and Crafts manner in dark stone by Robert Tischler, architect to the Volksbund Deutsche Kriegsgräberfürsorge, the German counterpart to the War Graves Commission, which had been established in 1919. The best examples are in Belgium, at Langemarck and at Vladslo. Inside the walls, the graves are sometimes marked by rough stone crosses but many bodies lie under squares of

[98]

granite bearing perhaps eight names on each. The cemeteries are often planted with oaks, associated with Thor, the god of war. These places were as carefully and subtly designed as the British war cemeteries and have a distinct stern, Teutonic character. One such is near Thiepval, at Fricourt, where some 17,000 casualties of the Battle of the Somme lie buried, with 11,970 of them in a mass grave. The cemetery was first created by the French authorities in 1920 and taken over by the Germans in 1929. It was not finished when the Second World War began, and the original wooden crosses over the graves were not replaced by thin dark metal crosses until 1977. (There were, of course, very many more German casualties on the Somme but, such was the hatred produced by the war, the French apparently destroyed thousands of bodies dumped in a quarry at Miraumont.) The cemetery at Vladslo is now known for the presence of the two figures of the *Trauernden Elternpaares* – the Mourning Parents – by Käthe Kollwitz, a great and powerful work of art originally placed in the nearby war cemetery at Roggeveld (since removed) in 1932. Kollwitz observed that, 'The British and Belgian cemeteries seem brighter, in a certain sense more cheerful and cosy, more familiar than the German cemeteries. I prefer the German ones. The war was not a pleasant affair; it isn't seemly to prettify with flowers the mass deaths of all these young men. A war cemetery ought to be sombre ...'

Most of the permanent British cemeteries were completed by the mid-1920s. As a feat of construction, this was a prodigious achievement, not least as the Commission's engineers had to construct foundations in unstable or waterlogged land, or in ground riddled with old trenches, dug-outs, craters and unexploded shells. Writing in 1937, Ware recorded that 'in France and Belgium alone there are 970 architecturally constructed cemeteries surrounded by 50 miles of walling in brick or stone, with nearly 1000 Crosses of Sacrifice and 560 Stones of Remembrance, and many chapels, record buildings and shelters; there are some 600,000 headstones resting on nearly 250 miles of concrete beam foundations. There are also eighteen larger memorials to those who have no known grave [...].' This was one of the largest schemes of public works ever undertaken, far larger than the contemporary achievement of the Office of Works erecting post offices and telephone exchanges (consistently neo-Georgian in style) back in Britain or the celebrated creation of new modern stations on the London Underground. Furthermore, high standards of design and construction were maintained despite increasing financial pressure as economic conditions worsened. Yet the work was surely cheap at the price. The total cost of *all* the Imperial War Graves Commission's cemeteries and memorials was £8,150,000, and to put this into perspective it is worth remembering that the Treasury's account for the so-called Third Battle of Ypres, that is, the horror of Passchendaele in 1917, was £22 million while just one day's shooting and shelling in September 1918 cost some £3.75 million. Sometimes it is cheaper as well as better to build rather than destroy.

Edmund Blunden, in his introduction to Fabian Ware's book *The Immortal Heritage*, published in 1937, wrote how visitors to the cemeteries 'must be impressed and even astonished at the degree of beauty achieved by the creators and guardians of these resting places. [...] The beauty, the serenity, the inspiration of the Imperial cemeteries have been frequently acknowledged by more able eulogists; for my part, I venture to speak of these lovely, elegiac closes (which almost cause me to deny my own experiences in the acres they now grace) as being after all the eloquent evidence against war. Their very flowerfulness and calm tell the lingerer that the men beneath that green coverlet should be there to enjoy such influence; the tyranny of war stands all the more terribly revealed.' Enough of the permanent cemeteries had been completed by 1922 to convince King George V that the Commission's principles were right when he and Queen Mary went on a pilgrimage to the battlefields. At the end, in the cemetery at Terlincthun outside Boulogne, in the shadow of the Colonne de la Grande Armée raised to the glory of Napoleon and commemorating the planned invasion of England, the King gave a speech in which he claimed that 'Never before in history have a people thus dedicated and maintained individual memorials to their fallen, and, in the course of my pilgrimage, I have many times asked myself whether there can be more potent advocates of peace upon earth through the years to come, than this massed multitude of silent witnesses to the desolation of war.'

5

MEMORIALS TO THE MISSING

Even with most of the Commission's war cemeteries completed, over half of the casualties remained uncommemorated: the Missing – those whose mutilated or burnt bodies were never identified, or who were blown to pieces, or lost at sea. Once the records had been gone through and the sums done, it emerged that there were over half a million of them: 517,000 men of the British Empire who had, in effect, disappeared between 1914 and 1918. The Commission's principles nevertheless held good and it was determined that every single missing man was to receive a permanent memorial. The question was how. The idea of 'false graves' – headstones with no bodies beneath – was mooted, and rejected. Then if there were to be memorials bearing the names of the missing, were they to be organised by regiments, which was not popular with relatives of the dead, or by the geographical location of their death? It was at first decided to have the names of the missing carved on walls in eighty-five of the cemeteries.

In the end, the project for memorials to the missing was merged with a quite separate proposal for battlefield memorials endorsed by the government – something with which Ware did not want the Commission to become involved. In 1919 a National Battlefield Memorial Committee was set up under the chairmanship of the Earl of Midleton. This soon encountered difficulties and it became clear that there was a danger of wasting taxpayers' money by duplicating memorials in particular places as well as having too many of them. The situation was further complicated by the desire of the Dominion governments to erect their own memorials in France and Belgium. When, in 1921, the Commission was asked to handle land negotiations for the proposed battlefield memorials, it seemed more sensible for these memorials to be combined with memorials for the missing. The Midleton Committee was dissolved and, for the first time, the War Graves Commission considered building large architectural monuments.

There were now to be a dozen large memorials to the missing erected in France and Belgium. Others were to be at Gallipoli, Jerusalem and Port Tewfik on the Suez Canal (all eventually designed by Burnet and Tait), in Basra (by Warren) and in Macedonia (by Lorimer). There were also those to commemorate men lost at sea (memorials at Chatham, Portsmouth and Plymouth were designed by Lorimer, and the Mercantile Marine Memorial at Tower Hill by Lutyens). At Kenyon's suggestion, each of the Commission's Principal Architects was to be given the opportunity to design a memorial while the design of the other memorials was to be decided by competitions. That for the memorial at La Ferté-sous-Jouarre, commemorating the Battle of the Marne, was to be limited to the Commission's Assistant Architects (and was won by Goldsmith).

The first and, in the end, the best-known of the Commission's memorials was built at Ypres – 'Wipers' – the ancient, smashed Flemish city whose stubborn defence for four years was inextricably associated with the horror and tragedy of the war in the public mind. The Ypres Salient was the graveyard for a quarter of a million British dead and in 1919 Winston Churchill announced that 'I should like us to acquire the whole of the ruins of Ypres' as a memorial, for 'A more sacred place for the British race does not exist in the world' – an idea which, not surprisingly, found little favour with its long-suffering and displaced citizens. That same year, Reginald Blomfield was invited by the government to survey sites in Ypres for a memorial and he recommended the spot where the seventeenth-century Menin Gate by the great French military engineer Vauban had once stood and the road into the city passed over a moat and between ramparts. By 1922 Blomfield's project for the Menin Gate had developed into a Memorial to the Missing containing a Hall of Memory. Work began on building it the following year as, all around, a passable re-creation of pre-war Ypres (today Ieper) was slowly rising.

For Blomfield, the Menin Gate was one of three works he wanted to be remembered by and 'perhaps the only building I have ever designed in which I do not want anything altered'. The most conservative as well as the oldest of the Commission's architects, he designed a new gateway between the ramparts which was long enough for a noble vaulted stone hall to contain the names of tens of thousands of Missing on its walls. At either end, inspired by Vauban and informed by his knowledge of French Classical architecture, Blomfield created a grand arched entrance articulated by a giant Roman Doric order. Above the parapet of the arch facing outwards from the city he placed a massive lion modelled by William Reid Dick: 'not fierce and truculent, but patient and enduring, looking outward as a symbol of the latent strength and heroism of our race'.

17. An aerial view of the Menin Gate at Ypres, designed by Sir Reginald Blomfield, at the time of its formal inauguration in 1927.

Perhaps it was the slight triumphalist air created by this feature which encouraged Siegfried Sassoon angrily to dismiss the whole thing as 'a pile of peace-complacent stone'. Sassoon, who knew well enough what the Ypres Salient had actually been like, wrote his poem 'On Passing the New Menin Gate' soon after it had been inaugurated with much ceremony in 1927 as the first and most important of the Commission's Memorials to the Missing. 'Was ever an immolation so belied / As these intolerably nameless names? / Well might the Dead who struggled in the slime / Rise and deride this sepulchre of crime.' But this justifiably cynical interpretation perhaps needs to be set against the reaction of the Austrian writer (and pacifist) Stefan Zweig, whose article on the Menin Gate published in 1928 in a Berlin newspaper Blomfield was pleased to quote in his *Memoirs of an Architect*: 'It is a memorial [...] offered not to victory but to the dead – the victims – without any distinction, to the fallen Australians, English, Hindus and Mohammedans who are immortalised to the same degree, and in the same chambers, in the same stone, by virtue of the same death. Here there is no image of the King, no mention of victories, no genuflection to generals of genius, no prattle about Archdukes and Princes: only a laconic, noble inscription – *Pro Rege Pro Patria*. In its really Roman simplicity this monument to the six and fifty thousand is more impressive than any triumphal arch or monument to victory that I have ever seen ...' This was surely a response which fully justified the tolerant and eirenic vision of the Imperial War Graves Commission.

In the event, although some 57,000 names were carved in the Hall of Memory and on the walls of the higher lateral galleries facing the ramparts, the Menin Gate proved to be nowhere near large enough to commemorate all those who disappeared in the mud of the Salient. A further 37,000 names – mainly of those who perished at Passchendaele – had to be carved on the long, curving colonnaded wall of stone and knapped flint which Herbert Baker designed to frame the large Tyne Cot war cemetery at Zillebeke. This cemetery was so called as a Newcastle regiment had nicknamed the strong German reinforced concrete blockhouses 'Tyne cottages' – one, at the suggestion of King George V, being retained to serve as the base for the Cross of Sacrifice. But by the time this cemetery and memorial was completed, the Commission's plans for Memorials to the Missing had undergone a crisis and had to be completely rethought.

The French were not at all happy about the memorials foreign governments proposed to erect on their territory. Concern was being expressed in local newspapers – particularly about the scale of the American memorials – and questions were being asked in the Assemblée Nationale. In 1926, it was reported that 'the French authorities were disquieted by the number and scale of the Memorials which the Commission proposed to erect in France and that some modification of the proposals was necessary'. This disquiet had resulted in the Commission des Monuments Historiques reporting adversely on the proposals for Memorials to the Missing at Béthune, St Quentin and the Faubourg d'Amiens Cemetery in Arras. Lutyens had been asked in 1923 to design a memorial at St Quentin to accommodate 60,000 names, later reduced to 30,000, and had come up with the multiple-arch concept which would eventually be realised at Thiepval. Here it was to be almost 180 feet high and the principal arch was to straddle a road – an idea no doubt suggested by Blomfield's Menin Gate – but the Corps des Ponts et Chaussées had objected to this. At Arras, Lutyens proposed an extraordinary tall, thin arch, 124 feet high, as a memorial to missing airmen; its sides were to consist of a vertical series of diminishing blocks, each pierced by an arched tunnel arranged on alternate axes and filled with bells which would swing and toll with the wind.

In April 1926, Major A. L. Ingpen, the Secretary-General of the Anglo-French Mixed Committee established in 1918 to smooth the diplomacy required by the Commission's work, explained the problem to Ware. 'The Commission des Monuments Historiques is of the opinion that the designs submitted are somewhat exaggerated, and too grandiose. Further, and in view of the fact that, owing to the present financial conditions in France, the French Government can do nothing to commemorate their own missing, such grandiose monuments will not be understood, or appreciated, by the general public, and may give rise to hostile comment, not only of an international character, but also against the Commission des Monuments Historiques itself for having approved such grandiose schemes put forward by a foreign government, for execution on French territory.' Ingpen feared that to raise a colossal arch at St Quentin would seem, 'in the eyes of the public, to be unreasonably obtrusive', especially in a place where the French had sustained as severe, if not greater, losses. Ware was not unsympathetic to this argument, for France was suffering even more than Britain from the losses of the war and from the huge cost of reconstructing the great swathe of country devastated by the fighting, and he replied that 'The attitude of the Commission des Monuments Historiques does not surprise me; indeed, the

18. The interior of the Thiepval Memorial lined with some of the 73,000 names of the Missing with the giant stone wreaths enclosing the names of Somme 'battles' placed above.

only complaint one can offer about it is that it was not made known to us earlier.' Others agreed, not least Lord Crewe, British Ambassador to France, who informed Ware 'how strongly I feel that expensive and ostentatious Memorials are out of place in this country […]'.

Ware had to use all his diplomatic skills to 'prevent a heap of trouble' and 'a first class row'. He was particularly anxious to stop the Monuments Historiques formally reporting to the French Foreign Office that it opposed the memorials at Arras and Vimy Ridge and 'the imposing and beautiful memorial of Lutyens's at St Quentin'. The whole matter was discussed by the Anglo-French Mixed Committee and it was eventually agreed that proposed memorials at St Quentin, Cambrai, Béthune, Lille and Pozières should be abandoned and that, instead of twelve memorials, there would now only be four in France and two in Belgium. The names of the Missing which could not be accommodated on these purpose-built memorials would be transferred to smaller memorials to be erected in existing war cemeteries. The proposed memorial at Lille, for which H. C. Bradshaw had won a competition, was therefore taken over the Belgian frontier to the cemetery at Ploegsteert. Bradshaw had also won the competition for the memorial at Cambrai and this was now transferred to Louverval cemetery. Similarly, J. R. Truelove designed memorials within existing cemeteries at Vis-en-Artois and Le Touret. Some of the names intended for several memorials on the Somme were transferred to a memorial colonnaded wall designed by W. H. Cowlishaw at Pozières cemetery and Herbert Baker designed a memorial in Dud Corner cemetery at Loos (so called because of the number of unexploded shells found there) to replace the memorial intended for Béthune.

19. The Thiepval Memorial from the west, with the graves of the 300 unknown French soldiers in the Anglo-French cemetery below the terrace.

At Arras, Lutyens's proposal for the Faubourg d'Amiens cemetery was completely redesigned on a less grandiose scale.

What remained to be established were the locations of the four new memorials in France. Land had already been acquired at Soissons for the rather pedestrian memorial by V. O. Rees with three stiff figures of soldiers by Eric Kennington. The contract for Goldsmith's memorial at La Ferté had already been acquired and work had started on Baker's Indian memorial at Neuve-Chapelle. That left but one memorial to replace the one at St Quentin and the two intended for the Somme battlefield, at the Butte de Warlencourt and between Contalmaison and Pozières (which was to have been designed by Baker). It was decided that this – now the only battlefield memorial to be built in France – must be on the Somme, and at Thiepval.

In July 1926 Lutyens was asked to consider moving his St Quentin design to Thiepval Ridge. That same month Ware was in Paris and told Crewe of his idea for a 'Campo Santo at Thiepval' with a common burial place for the bodies of both British and French unknown soldiers – an idea that was eventually realised. In order to get the French authorities to approve of the Memorial to the Missing of the Somme being built at Thiepval, Ware was keen to emphasise its Anglo-French significance and the following year he advanced the proposition that it should bear the inscription 'Aux armées Française et Britannique l'Empire Britannique reconnaissant' – a form of words evidently inspired by that on the portico of the Panthéon in Paris: 'Aux Grands Hommes La Patrie Reconnaissante'. Lord Crewe notified Paul Painlevé, the Minister of War, of this and was able to report that 'it gave the French very great pleasure'. (Kipling, as the Commission's literary adviser, was keen that 'The Missing of the Somme' should remain the principal inscription on the Memorial.)

Meanwhile, on 11 October 1926, Lutyens had visited Thiepval to discuss the design with E. Pontremoli, Inspecteur Général des Bâtiments Civils et des Palais Nationaux. Lutyens had been a party to moving the monument from St Quentin and, in August, had personally selected the new site at Thiepval with Pontremoli. He now brought with him 'an elaborate set of plans' which showed that what was now proposed was essentially his final design for St Quentin 'though with a return to the larger scale which the Architect originally had in view. There are minor modifications, involved in the monument not in its new setting straddling a road, and other modifications to meet Mons. Pontremoli's views […].' The following month Ware went with Lutyens to France to meet both Pontremoli and General de Castelnau, the chairman of the Anglo-French Mixed Committee, and was able to report to Rudyard Kipling that the encounter was 'extremely cordial' and 'resulted in complete agreement'. Kipling replied, thanking him for 'the news of the successful issue of your intrigue with the French *and* Lutyens. It isn't an embassy that *I* would care to have chaperoned.'

It would, however, take almost another two years before the formal approvals were finally granted, and this was after more of what Ware described as 'long and very difficult negotiations'. Difficulties were encountered in acquiring the land, partly because the site lay in the 'Zone Rouge', that is, the most devastated area of northern France, which was also dangerous because of unexploded shells and bombs. In such places, as Ingpen reported, there was an 'enormous number of formalities that have to be complied with' under special laws. 'The great difficulty has been,' he reported to Ware, 'to get any responsible person to make the final decision as they were all afraid of being accused of exceeding their powers' and he had to cope with 'a deal of somewhat flatulent verbosity'. In November 1927, the necessary land was secured from the French government – but only on a lease for eighteen years at first and not in perpetuity, as was normally the case with the Commission's cemeteries.

But there was possibly more than bureaucracy behind these delays. 'There may not be, and I hope is not, anything in my suspicion about the Somme Anglo-French Memorial,' Ware wrote to Ingpen in March 1927, 'but it is rather uncanny the way this thing keeps pace, so to speak, with our Thiepval business. The free lance, who is working this for the Foreign Office in the matter, has now sent me a letter he has had from the French Foreign Office saying that they had approached the Ministry of Beaux Arts with regard to the Anglo-French Memorial and telling him that General de Castelnau and Monsieur Pontremoli were already dealing with another Anglo-French Memorial and that they did not think there should be two separate memorials so close together.' Exactly what this second Anglo-French Memorial project was is not clear. Several years earlier, another architect, Sir John Simpson, had been sent to France to discuss a proposed joint memorial to the French and British missing of the Somme to be built near Amiens. This was soon abandoned and the British withdrew from the project, leaving the French to proceed with their own memorial at Notre-Dame de Lorette.

Ware asked Lord Crewe to put pressure on the French War Ministry, but in August Lutyens was still writing to

Ware that 'I long to hear about Thiepval.' In the same letter he also wrote that 'It is very kind of you to have written me so kindly regarding the Arras monument. I like pats on the back.' Eventually, in January 1928, the design for Thiepval was submitted to the Ministère de l'Instruction Publique et des Beaux-Arts. The following month, Ingpen explained to Ware that 'the Commission des Monuments Historiques sits to exercise a discretion on a question of taste, as the result of which they have already once refused Sir Edwin Lutyens's design, and it remains to be seen whether they will not accept it after slight modifications in accordance with the suggestions of Monsieur Pontremoli [...]'. Permission was eventually granted by the Commission on 12 April 1928. A year later, in a decree dated 24 April 1929, the Ministère de la Guerre authorised the erection of what some British newspapers were calling 'the Menin Gate of France', but by this date construction work at Thiepval had at long last begun.

6

....

THIEPVAL

There could not have been a more appropriate location for the Memorial to the Missing of the Somme than Thiepval. Occupying a commanding position on the German front line overlooking the valley of the Ancre, the place had been heavily fortified and most stubbornly defended during the Battle of the Somme and the slopes to its west saw some of the most ferocious fighting and the greatest loss of life of the campaign. Although less than half a mile from the British forward trenches on 1 July 1916, it was almost three months before the blasted ground where the village had once stood was finally captured, while the Germans on Thiepval Ridge to the north held out for even longer. Edmund Blunden, who was serving nearby, later recalled that 'This name Thiepval began to have as familiar and ugly a ring as any place ever mentioned by man.' The fields which now lie around the Somme Memorial were consecrated in blood.

Thiepval, one of the larger villages in the Somme district, had been damaged in 1870 during the Franco-Prussian War and its church had burned down. The German army came again on 27 September 1914, when the village and the ridge to its north were occupied as part of the outflanking movements which took place after the Battle of the Marne. The first casualty in Thiepval occurred that day, when a local farmer was

20. Thiepval *château* depicted in wartime postcards: *Top* – as it was before 1914; *Bottom* – under German occupation before the July 1916 offensive, already partly ruined by British shells.

shot, but by the French in error. That evening, the Germans occupied the *château*, which, for a while, made a fine officers' mess. The last Comte de Bréda, who owned most of the village and the surrounding farmland, had died earlier that year and been buried in the family vault in the chapel; the Comtesse had then locked up the *château* and left.

The Germans dug in on the high ground overlooking the Ancre, facing the French army below. At first this was a generally quiet sector on the Western Front compared with further north and east, and both sides were generally content to live by *laissez-faire*. British troops replaced the French in the trenches in the late summer of 1915. By the time the Somme offensive was launched ten months later, the *château* had long since ceased to be used as an officers' mess and had been reduced to a ruin by British shelling. During the winter of 1915–16 and especially after the arrival of Major von Fabeck, Hindenburg's nephew, in April 1916, the Germans strengthened and deepened their defences. It was now clear that an attack was threatened. Shell-proof bunkers were dug deep into the chalk and reinforced with concrete. Often thirty feet or more below the ground, these usually had more than one exit and were connected by a network of tunnels. Fortified machine-gun posts or pill-boxes covered every inch of land over which an assault might be launched. The Germans, as elsewhere along the Western Front, built solidly and well. When the foundations for the Thiepval memorial were being dug in May 1929 to a depth of twenty-four feet to rest on solid chalk, steps to three German dug-outs were discovered, still equipped with boxes of unexploded bombs and shells.

Edmund Blunden inspected these fortifications soon after this village fortress finally fell. 'Of all the strange artifices of war,' he later recalled in his *Undertones of War*, 'Thiepval was then a huge and bewildering repository. The old German front line west of it still retained its outline, after torrents of explosive which it had swallowed month after month. Steel rails and concrete had there been used with that remorseless logic which might be called real imagination, had been combined and fixed, reduplicated and thickened until the trench was as solid as a pyramid. In front of it here and there were concealed concrete emplacements, formerly lurking in the weeds and flowers of No Man's Land; beneath it [...] were prodigious dugouts, arranged even in two storeys, and in the lower storey of one of these was a little door in the wall. Opening, one went steadily descending along dark galleries, soon discovering that the stacks of boxes which seemed to go on for ever were boxes of explosives; then one arrived at two deep well-shafts, with wind-lasses and buckets ready for further descent [...]. In another great dugout were elaborate surgical appliances and medical supplies; another, again, was a kind of quartermaster's store [...]. The smell of the German dugouts was peculiar to them, heavy and clothy. There was, moreover, one vault here which was arrayed with mirrors, no doubt collected from the château whose white ruin still revealed the interior of a cellar, and on which an image of the Virgin was dreaming in the sullen daylight.'

The elaborate defences in and around the village and *château* at Thiepval were part of a wider complex of fortifications. To the north, at the western end of Thiepval Ridge, facing Thiepval Wood below (which was just behind the British front line), was the notorious Schwaben Redoubt, the strongest German position on the Somme. To defend Thiepval from the south, behind the German first line of defence, was a strong point called the *Wunderwerk*. And south of that, occupying another spur overlooking the Ancre and just north of Authuille, was the formidable Leipzig Redoubt. In short, Thiepval was an impregnable fortress, and it was against these carefully designed and constructed defences that British troops were ordered to advance, walking uphill, on 1 July 1916.

The position of these defences, if not their depth and strength, was known to the British as the ascendancy established by the Royal Flying Corps in the summer of 1916 allowed every section of the front to be photographed from the air. The massive artillery bombardment which preceded the assault was intended to destroy them. It failed to do so, but the torrent of high explosive made conditions hellish for those German troops not withdrawn from the front line. Sheltering beneath the Wunderwerk, Freiwilliger Eversmann recorded on 25 June, 'The barrage has now lasted thirty-six hours. How long will it go on?' And later, 'Veritable *Trommelfeuer*. In twelve hours shelling they estimate that 60,000 shells have fallen on our battalion sector. [...] When will they attack? Tomorrow or the day after? Who knows?' And in the early morning of the 27th, 'By 6 o'clock the fire had increased and soon we had a headache. But sit tight, it cannot last much longer. They say their munitions will soon be done. [...] There must be an end sometime to this horrible bombardment.' Finally, 'It is night. Shall I live till morning? Haven't we had enough of this frightful horror? Five days and five nights now this hell concert has lasted. One's head is like a madman's; the tongue sticks to the roof of the mouth. Almost nothing to eat and nothing to drink. No sleep. All contact with the outer world cut off. No sign of life from

KAMPF UM THIEPVAL —

A. H.

21. The Battle for Thiepval being observed from the German lines by Lieut-General Theodor von Wunde, in command of the Würtemberg 51 Reserve Infantry Brigade, drawn by his artist Albert Heim, 1916.

home nor can we send any news to our loved ones. What anxiety they must feel about us. How long is this going to last?'

It lasted until the early morning of 1 July. Then, at 7.30 a.m., the British advance began. What happened that day on the rising ground before Thiepval, and during the terrible weeks that followed, has been analysed and described in detail by Gerald Gliddon in his *When the Barrage Lifts*. In essence, the 36th (Ulster) Division attacked the Schwaben Redoubt to the north while further south the German lines from Thiepval down to the Leipzig Redoubt were the objective of the 32nd Division. Casualties were huge and to little gain. Emerging from Thiepval Wood, the Ulstermen managed to storm the Schwaben Redoubt and reach as far as the Stuff Redoubt and the second German line of defence – a distance of almost a mile – but the gains could not be held as there was no support and the survivors were repulsed by German counter-attacks. Attacks by the 15th & 16th Lancashire Fusiliers (the 1st & 2nd Salford Pals) and by the 16th Northumberland Fusiliers (the Newcastle Commercials) on Thiepval itself achieved nothing except to cover the ground with corpses. As even the *British Official History* observed, 'only bullet-proof soldiers could have taken Thiepval this day'. The only success achieved by the 32nd Division on 1 July was further south, where the 17th Highland Light Infantry (the Glasgow Commercials) succeeded in taking, and holding, part of the Leipzig Redoubt.

Many of the Ulster Division had belonged to the Ulster Volunteer Force which, only two years earlier, had been prepared to rebel against Asquith's government and resist the implementation of Home Rule for Ireland. On 1 July, which happened to be the anniversary of the Battle of the Boyne, they accomplished a remarkable feat of arms. Four VCs were won, but the losses amounted to some 5,500 – well over half of the total British casualties at Thiepval that day. No wonder that the home of the Ulster Division in Lisburn was renamed the Thiepval Barracks; no wonder that the memorial to the Ulster Division was raised at Thiepval. Standing less than a mile to the north-west of the Memorial to the Missing of the Somme, it is a replica of Helen's Tower near Bangor in County Down, a Victorian folly-tower designed by William Burn and built by the Marquess of Dufferin and Ava on his Clandeboye estate, below which the Ulster Division drilled before being sent out to France.

F. P. Crozier, then commanding a battalion of Ulstermen, later described that terrible morning in his book, *A Brass Hat in No Man's Land*. 'Again I look southward from a different angle and perceive heaped up masses of British corpses on the German wire in front of the Thiepval stronghold, while live men rush forward in orderly procession to swell the weight of numbers in the spider's web. Will the last available and previously detailed man soon appear to do his futile duty unto death on the altar of sacrifice? […] The battalion is now formed up lying down on the road. They are enfiladed from Thiepval village while field guns open up on them from the front. They can't stay here. […] And what of the dead and wounded? This spirited dash across no man's land, carried out as if on parade, has cost us some fifty dead and seventy disabled. The dead no longer count. War has no use for dead men. With luck they will be buried later; the wounded try to crawl back to our lines. […] Meanwhile I mount the parapet to observe. The attack on the right has come to a standstill; the last detailed man has sacrificed himself on the German wire to the God of War. Thiepval village is masked with a wall of corpses.' Finally, 'The net result of the barren, glorious bloody battle of Thiepval is that over seven hundred men of the West Belfast battalion of the Royal Irish rifles prove their ability to subordinate matter to mind. Intellectual discipline had triumphed.'

Over the following three bloody months, Thiepval, despite being pounded with constant shelling, remained resolutely in German hands. The high ground here was regarded as the key to the defence of Bapaume and every British advance was met by a ferocious counter-attack. The front here hardly advanced at all. Thiepval was stubbornly defended by the Württemberger 180th Regiment of the 26th Reserve Division, which had been garrisoned here ever since September 1914. This long retention of the same position by a single German unit was without parallel elsewhere and, as even official British accounts recognised, the Württembergers, assisted by Prussians of the 99th Reserve Infantry Regiment, made it a point of honour to hold Thiepval at all costs. Gradually, however, the British advanced south of Thiepval, leaving the village and the ridge beyond besieged from the west and south. More of the Leipzig Redoubt was taken on 7 July and the remainder of this salient was captured on 24 August by the 25th Division. Mouquet Farm, further to the east, was taken by the Australians on 15 September.

The final assault on Thiepval, by British and Canadian troops of the 18th Division, was made on 25 September after another massive artillery bombardment and what remained of the village, together with the Zollern Redoubt to the east, was taken the following day (there is a small memorial to the 18th Division just to the north of Lutyens's memorial).

The fighting was desperate, with the Germans defending with machine-gun fire from their concealed positions and the British taking each trench and dug-out with bombs and grenades. British casualties were about 1,500. The advance was assisted by the advent of two of the new British tanks, nicknamed '*Crème de Menthe*' and '*Cordon Bleu*', one of which emerged from Thiepval Wood to deal with some of the machine-gun positions on the site of the *château* before getting bogged down in the ubiquitous mud. The following year, John Masefield recorded how one tank 'charged an enemy trench here. It plunged and stuck fast and remained in the mud, like a giant animal stricken dead in its spring. It was one of the sights of Thiepval during the winter, for it looked most splendid; afterwards it was salved and went to fight again.' This mud, which Masefield thought 'will be remembered by our soldiers long after they have forgotten the shelling, was worse at Thiepval than elsewhere, or, at least, could not have been worse elsewhere. The road through Thiepval was a bog, the village a quagmire.'

Lyn Macdonald has written how 'The Germans fought to the death for Thiepval – for every inch of trench dug deep into the pulverised rubble, for every strong-point hidden in the old vaults and cellars, for every gallery and dugout burrowed into the chalk. One by one they were overwhelmed. When night fell the few who were left were still fighting to retain a last foothold in the north-western corner of Thiepval village. The British infantry paused, drew breath and attacked again in the morning. Before the sun rose through the thick autumn mist, Thiepval was finally captured.' But even then the Germans held out in the Schwaben Redoubt and along Thiepval Ridge and the higher ground to the north and only on 14 October were they finally cleared from the Redoubt. When Haig finally declared the Somme offensive over, on 18 November, Grandcourt, little more than two miles to the north-west of Thiepval, was still within the German front line.

Earlier that month, Edmund Blunden was at Thiepval. 'We took over that deathtrap known as the Schwaben Redoubt, the way to which lay through the fallen fortress of Thiepval. One had heard the worst accounts of the place, and they were true. Crossing the Ancre again [...], one went up through the scanty skeleton houses of Authuille, and climbing the dirty little road over the steep bank, one immediately entered the land of despair. Bodies, bodies, and their useless gear heaped the gross waste ground; the slimy road was soon only a mud track which passed a whitish tumulus of ruin with lurking entrances, some spikes that had been pinetrees, a bricked cellar or two, and died out. The village pond, so blue on the map, had disappeared. The Ligne de Pommiers had been grubbed up. The shell-holes were mostly small lakes of what was no doubt merely rusty water, but had a red and foul semblance of blood.'

In his book on *The Old Front Line* published the following year after the Germans had retreated to the Hindenburg line, John Masefield described what remained at Thiepval. 'Where the shattered hillside slopes towards our lines,' he wrote, 'there are remnants of trees [...]. All are burnt, blasted and killed. One need only glance at the hill on which they stand to see that it has been more burnt and shell-smitten than most parts of the lines. It is as though the fight here had been more than to the death, to beyond death, to the bones and skeleton of the corpse which was yet unkillable.

This is the site of the little hill village of Thiepval, which once stood at a crossroads here among apple orchards and the trees of a park. It had a church, […] and a fine seigneurial château, in a garden, beside the church; otherwise it was a little lonely mean place, built of brick and plaster on a great lonely heap of chalk downland. […] The road is reddish with the smashed bricks of the village. Here and there in the mud are perhaps three courses of brick where a house once stood […]. Blasted, dead, pitted stumps of trees, with their bark in rags, grow here and there in a collection of vast holes, ten feet deep and fifteen feet across, with filthy water in them. There is nothing left of the church; a long reddish mound of brick, that seems mainly powder round a core of cement, still marks where the château stood.' (Later in 1917, a satirical article in *Punch* magazine intended for Tommies advertised 'Pratt's tours of the Front' – 'Don't miss it, you may never see another war' – with such attractions as a 'Lantern Lecture by Captain Crump at Thiepval château'.)

On 25 March 1918, Thiepval was back in German hands as Ludendorff's offensive at a stroke rendered pointless the huge sacrifices made to capture the high ground east of the Ancre, although the advance did not get far beyond Albert. More heavy casualties ensued. The following 24 August the site of the village was recaptured, apparently without the loss of a single man. After the war, Thiepval, obliterated and depopulated, lay in the Zone Rouge. In 1920, the illustrated *Michelin Guide to the Battle-Fields* devoted to the Somme recorded that 'Everything was pounded to bits by the shells. Of the onetime flourishing village, nothing remains. A shapeless mass of broken stones marks the site of the Castle. The place has become a desolate waste overrun with weeds and grass. Here

22. 'Blasted, dead, pitted stumps of trees': all that remained of the village of Thiepval when the fighting was over.

and there traces of the defence-works: redoubts, trenches etc., and the graves of British and German soldiers, conjure up visions of the bloody struggle which took place here.'

With the fighting over, the local population began to move back and attempted to return to life as before, although before this could happen bodies had to be exhumed and live munitions disposed of. One veteran of the Somme, R. H. Royle, now an Anglican curate, returned in 1919 and found that 'the scene is not without a brighter side. Within a mile of poor devastated Thiepval, shell holes have been filled in, barbed wire removed and trenches blocked up. Already the French peasants were reaping their harvest, back once more in their own part of beloved France, living like foxes in holes in the ground, old Nissen huts, trench shelters – anywhere, but full of joy at being home again after nearly five years of exile.' At first, however, it was proposed not to rebuild the village; instead, the commune was to be abolished and partitioned, so that Thiepval would have joined the twenty-five places which disappeared from the map of the Somme area after the war. In the event, strong local protests ensured that Thiepval rose again. The new church, designed by C. A. Dory (who would design the Picardy pavilion at the 1937 Exposition in Paris), was completed in 1932 but the *château* was not rebuilt. The Comte de Bréda, who had died in 1914, was the last of the line and the site of his home is now a farm (near the church and north of the Somme Memorial). Nature, as always, soon healed many of the visible wounds; in 1932, a correspondent visiting Thiepval for the unveiling reported that 'it is almost impossible to tell that it was ever devastated by war. Fields of corn stand on the once blasted slopes of Thiepval hill [...].' The horrors lay below the surface, however, in buried

23. The Thiepval Memorial (being refaced) seen from the air in 1982, with the ghosts of former trenches and fortifications dug into the chalk still visible in the surrounding fields.

fortifications and dug-outs where many bodies still lie, and even today, in certain conditions, the lines of the trenches can be detected in the surrounding farmland.

....

7

THE DESIGN

Lutyens first proposed building the Memorial to the Missing of the Somme on the brow of the hill at Thiepval, overlooking the valley of the Ancre. H. F. Robinson, the Commission's Director of Works, visited Thiepval with him in September 1928 and reported that 'Sir Edwin had no doubt whatever that the site he had selected from the survey and levels [...] was by far the best. [...] Sir Edwin will consider other positions which, however, he asked me to say he would only do most reluctantly.' In the end, however, he had to bow to the wishes of the Finance Committee, which was stressing the need for economy. By January 1929 the site had been moved from the brow of the hill to nearer its summit, on land which had belonged to the park of the *château*, so there was no need for 'a high and expensive podium' and the access road could be reduced in length (back in 1926 Pontremoli had pressed the Commission to take more land than Lutyens specified so that an avenue or vista could lead from Thiepval village). At one stage, Lutyens apparently proposed that – as with the St Quentin project – the memorial should straddle the Thiepval–Authuille road.

Lutyens also had to reduce the size of the memorial yet again. He had earlier had to scale down the design of the St Quentin memorial when the number of names was reduced from 60,000 to 30,000; now the Finance Committee proposed to reduce his final design for Thiepval either by one eighth or by a quarter – which was agreed. Reduction by 25 per cent brought its height slightly below that of the Arc de Triomphe, which would be 'not displeasing to the French authorities who had approved the original design'. This scaling down was approved by Frederic Kenyon, who was sure that this was 'not sacrificing the dignity of the memorial'. Poor Lutyens was by now used to this: as well as having had to reduce the St Quentin design in size, he had had to scale down his first design for Viceroy's House back in 1913 and recently had to do the same with his project for the British Embassy in Washington, DC.

A level podium was, however, still required as the final site selected slopes gently down towards the river. To the west, therefore, a brick terrace rises some twenty feet above the cemetery containing the graves of the French and British unknown soldiers. To the east, this level podium is extended as retaining walls supporting a forecourt, meeting the rising ground where the principal open axis crosses the access road from Thiepval village. The basement of the memorial itself was also extended to the east as walls on the podium containing the forecourt lawn. Originally, these walls gently stepped down and then turned outwards to make a solid circular wall around the *rond point* or gravel roundel placed where the main axis crossed the access road (which was extended southwards as a farm road). This circular wall – broken by openings – disguised the oblique angle between the two axes by emphasising the centrality of this crucial forecourt space. Above this podium, flush with the retaining walls to north and south, Lutyens raised his memorial, with the largest arches framing the dominant east–west axis.

Lutyens had used the Classical round arch from almost the beginning of his career, and he had been interested in the Roman triumphal arch form ever since he first had the opportunity to design a memorial. This was back in 1911, when, on his visit to South Africa, he was asked to design the Rand Regiments Memorial in Johannesburg. Sited in Eckstein Park, it was a variation on the simple Roman arch theme. The principal arched opening rose into a pediment while lower arches penetrated the narrower side elevations. Above the main cornice was an attic storey with concave sides – a true Baroque feature – surmounted by a figure of Victory by the sculptor Naoum Aronson. The sides of the arches were carved with the names of the dead. As Christopher Hussey remarked, this 'design is interesting as the forerunner of some of his 1914–18 war memorials and the earliest demonstration of his pure classicism […]'.

This theme had been continued in the All India War Memorial arch in New Delhi, first proposed in 1917 and begun in 1921. Placed at the far end of the central axis, or Kingsway, from Viceroy's House, this memorial is of the Arc de Triomphe type except given a greater vertical emphasis. The design also exhibits much more dynamism than the French original as the principal cornice is much more prominent and the walls and piers are given a pronounced batter (or slope), while the arch itself appears to be sustaining a massive stepped attic. This attic, like that on the Rand Regiments Memorial, has concave sides and is surmounted by the shallow dome (intended to emit smoke) which appeared on the St Quentin design. A further important feature is that here the principal and subsidiary arches are logically connected, with the level of the keystone of the smaller arches at the sides being extended by a continuous cornice to become the springing of the larger arches on the main elevations. The same ideas were developed in the War Memorial in Victoria Park in Leicester, where the walls of the arched structure step back as it rises, and in the cenotaph pylons at the Etaples Military Cemetery.

For St Quentin, however, Lutyens arrived at a much more complex solution. This was probably stimulated by the need to find sufficient space for incorporating 60,000 names on the memorial. In consequence, Lutyens adopted the triple Roman triumphal arch model, such as those of Constantine and Septimius Severus, where smaller side arches flank a central arch. By adopting this type of elevation on all four sides rather than two, he no doubt realised that the inter-sections of three arched tunnels on two axes would create sixteen separate piers and thus provide large areas of inter-nal wall space: forty-eight panels on which to carve those 'intolerably nameless names'. Out of this concept he created a form entirely without precedent. Roman and Renaissance triumphal arches are essentially uni-directional gateways, even if the side elevations are pierced by a smaller arch. There had been arches which were 'quadrifrons', that is, with single arched openings in all four directions, but never before had a free-standing structure been proposed with multiple arched intersecting openings penetrating the mass on all four sides.

Lutyens developed two more novel ideas to generate the St Quentin design. One was to connect the intersecting arched passages in a geometrical hierarchy, with the keystone of the smallest arch being at the level of the springing of the next largest arch on the alternate elevation, and the height of the keystone of that being that of the springing of the next largest arch back on the original elevation, and so on. Four arches of ascending scale, each of the same proportions, were therefore logically unified while being aligned on intersecting axes. The second novel idea was to place each arched tunnel, whether small or large, within its own discrete cubic mass of masonry, and then to pile up these blocks into a pyramidal form rather than having all the tunnels penetrate one single rectangular block.

Such a shape could only have been conceived by an artist with an immediate and acute sense of three-dimensional form, with an ability to see 'in the round'. As always, Lutyens developed these ideas in his sketches – his means of developing and communicating complex architectural ideas. These sketches often took a 'worm's eye view' of a structure, emphasising the receding planes and thus its monumentality, and are comparable with the celebrated drawings by the great modern architect Erich Mendelsohn of imaginary projects made while he was in the trenches on the Eastern Front. Several sketches of complex pyramidal arch designs, which may have been either for St Quentin or for Arras, exist among Lutyens's surviving drawings in the collection of the Royal Institute of British Architects; some are added to geometrical drawings of the St Quentin design. Another drawing shows the arrangement of masses in an axonometric representation – a three-dimensional 'bird's eye' view drawn out on constant geometrical principles rather than in perspective. The essential conception together with the complex mathematics required seem to have been worked out between 1923, when the memorial was commissioned, and December 1924, when 'the War Graves Commission have accepted my St Quentin design with acclamation!' The final design is depicted in the sketch drawn on a sheet of Lutyens's office writing paper (with its telegraphic address: *'Aedificavi, London'* – 'I have built' – see page 58), which was probably made in a committee meeting or at a dinner table to illustrate his idea.

A half-inch to the foot scale model of the St Quentin Memorial was shown in the Architectural Room at the Royal Academy's Summer Exhibition in 1925. In its review, the *Builder* magazine thought the design 'monumental and dignified, finely proportioned and distinguished, but we do not like the union of brick and stone, and would have preferred all in brick if not all in stone and marble; we never get the extremist quality of breadth and power of effect in mixed materials'. This criticism was to ignore the purpose of the memorial in that it would not have been possible to carve tens of thousands of names into brickwork. More interesting, especially in view of the Liverpool Cathedral project which was to come a few years later, is Albert Richardson's reaction: 'From the design,' he wrote in the *Architectural Review*, 'it is possible to gather Sir Edwin Lutyens's idea of a church in section, open at the sides and ends. This memorial will have the effect of great scale and interesting perspective. It is to be built of brick and stone.'

It has been suggested by the American historian Vincent Scully and by others since that in his final, executed design for Thiepval, Lutyens was influenced by the proximity of the basilica of Notre-Dame-de-Brebières at Albert – the church whose precariously leaning giant statue of the Virgin and Child after German shelling became such a prominent and mythical landmark during the war. Also built of brick and stone, it had been designed by Edmond Duthoit in 1884 in a Byzantine-Romanesque style and had a triple-arched west

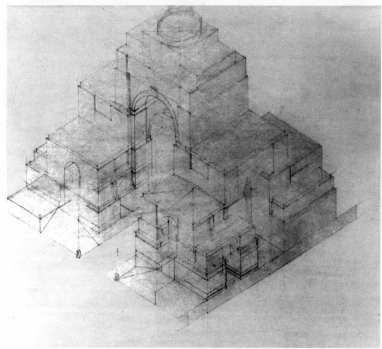

24. *Top* Typical perspective sketches by Lutyens developing his ideas
pencilled on one of his preliminary design drawings for the proposed
Memorial at St Quentin.
Bottom Complex geometry: an axonometric projection drawing of the St
Quentin arch design.

25. The timber model of the St Quentin design, painted red and white,
which was shown at the Royal Academy's Summer Exhibition in 1925.

portal with an upper arch above the central door under the tower. Reduced to a pile of rubble by British shells in April 1918, the building was being reconstructed to the original design by the architect's son, Louis Duthoit, when Lutyens was designing his memorial. But apart from the fact that Duthoit's basilica is an example of the sort of incoherent eclectic architecture that Lutyens loathed while churches with triple-arched western portals are commonplace, the idea that there was an influence is rendered absurd by the simple fact that the Memorial to the Missing design was first worked out for St Quentin, which is nowhere near Albert. As for the brick and stone, Lutyens was more likely to have had such precedents for Thiepval as Hampton Court in mind, designed by his hero, Wren. Besides, red brick is the ubiquitous building material in this part of France. 'Bricks!' Lutyens would write to A. G. Shoosmith, his brilliant representative in India, when, in 1928, he was designing his extraordinary brick Garrison Church in Delhi (one of the great buildings of the century and one in which the influence of the Somme Memorial may be traced). 'A building of one material is for some strange reason much more noble than one of many. It may be the accent it gives of sincerity, the persistence of texture and definite unity. [...] The Romans did it! Why should not Britons?'

The St Quentin design was eventually realised in most respects at Thiepval. The whole thing is extraordinarily difficult to describe in words; indeed, A. S. G. Butler, his dense analytical text in the *Lutyens Memorial* volume, would seem to have been defeated by it despite recounting its dimensions and proportional relationships. 'It is a matter of reciprocal and interwoven solid forms,' he observed, 'which can only be put into words tedious to read.' An attempt at descriptive analysis of its most complex form must be made here, even if reading this may also become tedious.

What was built at Thiepval between 1929 and 1932 was smaller than the original St Quentin design, being some 185 feet wide and 135 feet deep, and rising to that tactful height of 140 feet above the podium (although to some 160 feet above the ground), but the arrangement of arches was the same; the principal difference to the earlier project being the omission of the shallow dome over its summit. Each arch, although different in height and width, is of exactly the same proportion, that is, two and a half times high as it is wide, the largest having a span of thirty-five feet. Because the hierarchy of arches alternates on each face of the memorial, the four elevations present a composition of large central arches flanked by much smaller arches. Only on the diagonal can the architectural and proportional relationship between the series of four arches of different sizes be appreciated.

Nothing is simple here, however, and while the largest arch rises from the podium level, the three smaller arches rise from a higher level above a plinth – the level at which the Stone of Remembrance is placed. This may reflect the fact that in the original design the largest arch was to straddle a road. Nor are all the arches identical in form while differing in size. Lutyens did not merely enlarge the impost and archivolt mouldings as the dimensions increased, but, as Butler put it, 'multiplied their members on the basis of a standard two facets and one cavetto'. This was what Butler's draughtsman, Lutyens's former assistant George Stewart, 'describes as Sir Edwin's Family of Mouldings; and it is a mark of

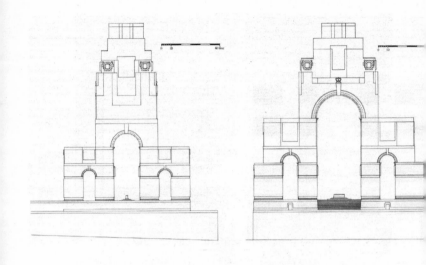

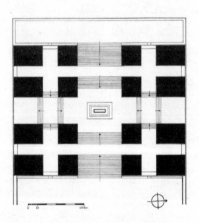

26. The front and side elevations and the plan of the Thiepval Memorial.

27. A diagonal view of Thiepval which shows the harmonic geometrical progression of the arches on two axes as well as the complexity of the build-up of masses.

his most advanced design'. Nor are these arches pure semi-circles; they are slightly depressed arches, or ellipses, and a surviving working drawing indicates exactly how the centring for the arches was to be set up. As with the Cenotaph, Lutyens employed optical corrections throughout the design. Subtleties abound. The flat surfaces carrying the endless names elide with plinth below and wall above across recessed mouldings – an example of Lutyens's concern with continuous wall planes. Then there is the attention to detail which humanises what might be an intimidating structure: the garland moulding of laurel and oak leaves placed above the upper pavement level, for instance, or the intriguing pattern of split spirals in stone and bricks which enhances the internal pavements and the terrace.

All such detail makes the experience of walking between the stone walls of names, exploring the succession of tunnels as they intersect, enjoyable as well as melancholy. And then there are the surprises. Look up, and the vaults which spring above the giant carved wreaths placed against the brick walls are not of the conventional Classical pattern, with the curved surface relieved by square indentations, or coffering. Lutyens looked elsewhere and, in an ecumenical gesture, took the Buddhist railing motif from Sanchi which he had wrapped around the dome of Viceroy's House, turned it inside out, up-ended it and made it cover his tunnel passages. As in New Delhi, there is a fusion here of East and West, if mostly West. But there is much more.

Everything described so far is explicable in terms of the Classical language of architecture. This is not, however, true of the exterior of the Memorial. Apart from the mouldings on the archivolts of the arches and the continuation of the recessed mouldings and garlands which frame the stone panels, the outside surfaces are severely unadorned until more wreaths and the carved stone Imperial crowns are reached at a high level on the tower. Nothing projects; there are only set-backs as the structure rises – enhanced by the curve and batter of *entasis* – leaving some surfaces to remain standing as piers. It is a composition of planes of masonry and of recessions. The lines of cornices which appear within the tunnels are continued only as flat stone bands above the brickwork. What matters are the set-backs, which are managed alternately according to Lutyens's personal sensibility: first on one elevation, then on the lateral elevation higher up as the mass rises and diminishes. Some of the recessions model planes of brickwork; others govern the disposition of the cubic masses of which the monument is composed. The smallest such building block contains the smallest arches on the side elevations. And arches are placed centrally in each block – except on the principal elevations to east and west where the lower, flanking blocks are extended outwards to create a buttressing effect. The Thiepval Memorial is not an arch but a tower of arches.

Butler described the whole thing as 'a solid geometrical composition of arches and their supports, more advanced than anything Lutyens had previously done towards complete abstraction'. It certainly has no connection with anything in the Classical canon, but it does have roots in the past. The pyramidal composition echoes the shape of the Pyramids of Egypt and other monuments of the Ancient World. Nor is this coincidence. The architecture of the West in the first third of the twentieth century was conspicuous for an interest in the abstraction and monumentality of early civilisations: Egypt,

Persia, India, Central and South America. Such monuments as the burial towers of Persia or the ziggurats of the Mayans had resonances with modern industrial forms. Indeed, in his 1934 book *The Romance of the Skyscraper*, Alfred Bossom, the British architect who had worked in the United States before becoming a Conservative MP, juxtaposed illustrations of a thirty-five-storey commercial building with 'The original American skyscraper': a thousand-year-old 230-foot high ziggurat with a monumental staircase at Tikal in Guatemala. Similarly, Lutyens's admirer Robert Byron pointed out that the eleventh-century brick tower at Gumbad-i-Kabus in Persia, which he considered one of the great buildings of the world, 'exhibits the principle of vertical mobility in design carried out with that merciless severity so fashionable in modern industrial architecture'.

Much architecture of the 1920s was characterised by the absence of projections and a stepped, receding profile. Such compositions were encouraged by American skyscraper designs, which themselves responded to the exigencies of the New York zoning laws of 1917, the result being 'in-stepping' at high levels. And Byron pointed out that ancient buildings in Lhassa, Angkor or Cairo had lessons to teach the modern architect coping with the new problem of the high building. Pyramidal or stepped profiles are to be found in many buildings of the 1920s and 1930s, such as the monumental towers of Sir Giles Gilbert Scott, or Charles Holden's Underground headquarters in London, or Herbert Rowse's ziggurat ventilation tower by the Mersey opposite Liverpool. But no architect handled such forms with quite as much architectural logic and intellectual control as Lutyens did at Thiepval. In being at once Classical and abstract, traditional and exotic, the Memorial to the Missing of the Somme was truly modern in its time.

Above the central arch, the memorial rises as a tower in a series of alternate steps to culminate in a final attic block with a flat top instead of the St Quentin saucer dome on a drum. Where earlier memorials had concave recessions in the Baroque manner, this attic is faceted with severe straight lines. There is no Classical precedent for this summit; it is reminiscent, if anything, of the top of an American Art Deco skyscraper. It has often been stated that the Great War marked a *caesura* between traditional forms of expression and modernism although, as Jay Winter argued in his study of *Sites of Memory, Sites of Mourning*, 'the war gave a new lease of life to a number of traditional languages expressed both conventionally and in unusual and modern forms'. This was certainly true of the work of the Imperial War Graves Commission, in which the language of Classicism was handled with conspicuous sophistication and intelligence, and thus communicated with a wide public. What is extraordinary about the Thiepval Memorial is that Lutyens succeeded in transcending that language and developed a form of expression which was at once timeless and conspicuously modern, creating a monument whose power to convey its terrible purpose continues to resonate across the years. As Roderick Gradidge has rightly claimed, at Thiepval, Lutyens adopted 'an entirely new three-dimensional approach to Classical architecture'.

Work on digging the foundations had begun by March 1929. The memorial is hollow, built of engineering brick with the large flat roofs created by the set-backs constructed of reinforced concrete. While the stone panels were of imported white Portland stone, other dressings were of

28. Building the Memorial at Thiepval in *c.*1930.

Massangis limestone and the facing brick was also French, from the Pérenchies Tile Works near Lille. This would later cause huge problems. A. J. Thomas, Lutyens's chief assistant, visited Thiepval in December 1929 and reported that 'the facing brick has been the subject of considerable anxiety, and the cause of a great deal of work, both in France and in London [...]'. In a subsequent letter, Thomas stressed 'the importance of keeping the mortar joints fully flushed on the face'. Lutyens visited the site in June 1931 and reported that 'Good progress has been made here and the monument grows and is nearing the springing [?] of the main arch for which the [centring?] is now being prepared.' He also reported that 'We decided to omit the Macadam road up to the monument from the round point and substitute grass in the forecourt. This will prove an economy and will add to the repose in the setting of the monument.'

The Somme Memorial at Thiepval was finished early in 1932, with those 73,357 names in lettering by Macdonald Gill carved into fifty-six stone wall panels (the eight external side panels were left bare). It was originally planned to have the official ceremony for what was described as the 'unveiling' on 16 May (it would surely have been rather difficult to veil a 140-foot-high monument). The dedication of the Memorial to the Missing in the Fauboug d'Amiens Cemetery at Arras – which Lutyens had redesigned on a more modest scale in 1927 with a colonnaded cloister enclosing a memorial to the missing of the Royal Flying Corps, the Royal Naval Air Service and the Royal Air Force – was planned for the same date. These ceremonies had to be postponed, however, owing to the assassination of the President of the French Republic, Paul Doumer, by a mad Russian. The Memorial to the Missing

29. The unveiling ceremony at Thiepval on 1 August 1932; the French Guard of Honour is drawn up in front.

of the Somme was at last inaugurated on the afternoon of
1 August by the Prince of Wales, the future King Edward
VIII, in the presence of the new French President, Albert
Lebrun. The ceremony, which was broadcast to listeners in
Britain by the BBC, emphasised the Anglo-French nature of
the memorial and of the struggle which had made it necessary. The Prince of Wales first inspected the French Guard
of Honour and music from both French and British military
bands was directed by Adrian Boult. Prayers were conducted
by two former British Army chaplains and by the Bishop
of Amiens. The official programme quoted the inscription
on the Cross of Sacrifice in the Thiepval Cemetery in both
English and French, 'That the world may remember the
common sacrifice of two and a half million dead, here have
been laid side by side Soldiers of France and of the British
Empire in eternal comradeship.'

By 1932, post-war optimism about the prospects for a
better world had been dissipated; the League of Nations
had failed to create international harmony and the economic
situation was almost as unstable as the political – in Britain
as well as France. Pacifism now seemed an idle dream, and,
only six months later – in January 1933 – Adolf Hitler would
become Chancellor of Germany. The official speeches were
nevertheless full of hope: delivered in front of a memorial to
tens of thousands of victims of war, they surely had to be. The
Prince of Wales said that, 'It is fitting that the crowning stone
of the work of our own Imperial War Graves Commission
should be laid in France; it is fitting that the last of their
Memorials should bear a tribute to the Armies of France as
well as to our own [...]. But these myriads of names carved
in stone and printed on almost endless pages must form no

mere Book of the Dead if, in the words which in honest faith we have cut deep and clear, they are to "live for evermore". They must be, and I believe they are, the opening chapter in a new Book of Life – the foundation and guide to a better civilization, from which war, with all the horror which our generation has added to it, shall be banished, and in which national bitterness and hate, selfishness and greed, shall flee abashed before the spirits of the dead.'

The French President's speech was eloquent but more sombre in tone. 'Here we find ourselves,' he said (to quote the translation in the War Graves Commission's files), 'on the territory of two unassuming and peaceful villages, Thiepval and Authuille, whose houses, all in mud plaster, timidly grouped themselves before 1914 round a humble belfry. Their inhabitants did not have any troubles but those of the sowing time and harvest. The battle destroyed Thiepval and Authuille to such an extent, that it was impossible, after the war, to find any trace of the villages. […] In spite of the magnificent reconstruction, this landscape is touched with infinite sadness. There is about a persistent memory of death. Death, in fact, for such a long time ruled these places and withered in their bloom with a pitiless scythe so many young men, full of promises and hope for the future.' Referring to King George V's speech at Terlincthun a decade earlier, President Lebrun continued, 'Let us listen as he asked us to do, let us listen to the lesson of the tombs, which comes from the immense city of the dead which is spread around us. It teaches us that War always brings with it horrors and that it is woeful and hateful, and that it is the duty of all men of good will to outlaw it for ever.'

The architect of the memorial was present on this occasion (he had not been invited to the unveiling of the first

30. Sir Fabian Ware talking to the Prince of Wales at the unveiling ceremony; Lutyens, in his 'Togs', is standing behind.

temporary Cenotaph). For some, this was a mixed blessing as he never stopped cracking jokes. The Earl of Crawford and Balcarres, chairman of the Royal Fine Art Commission (on which Lutyens sat), wrote afterwards that 'To have to laugh at every remark he makes (and they are all witty) – to have to do so incessantly (for he never stops talking for a moment) is the most fatiguing experience I know! One can't remember anything he says, and yet his conversation is brilliant – often wise, always vivacious; none the less his good spirits depress everybody – and one sees people getting quietly out of his way, simply because the effort of sympathetic laughter is overwhelming.' As his latest biographer, Jane Ridley, has suggested, 'Ned had become the sad comedian, hiding his unhappiness behind a mask of forced hilarity.'

Lutyens himself described the ceremony in a letter to his wife. The previous day he had been at the unveiling in Arras: 'My monument had a great success […] I wept a good deal – the speeches were short, the laying of wreaths quick and the hymns oh so slow […].' Afterwards he 'got out of Togs' and went off with two old generals, Claud Jacob and Hubert Gough, down to the Somme, ending up at Thiepval. 'They both had had commands and they went over – from car – the battle grounds – discovering and recognising old sites and area-hoods and redoubts. It was thrilling […]. Then I took the two generals up onto my monument. They were moved, which was embarrassing again, and "terribly" pleased with it, for which I was glad and very thankful. The sheds and tribunes for the morrow's function rather destroyed the approach but when you mounted the steps to the great stone under the great arch the wide battle area was framed by the series of arches – and the terrace overlooked the great French and

English cemetery.' As for the ceremony itself, he only commented that the Prince of Wales arrived and 'the photographers were odious, a great crowd of them, round the prince like flies around something nasty and oversweet'.

What, behind all the jokes and the socialising, Lutyens actually thought about the completion of his astonishing, poignant monument, we cannot now know. Certainly he could not have realised that the stupendous design he was then working on, which the interior of the Thiepval arch prefigured – Liverpool Metropolitan Cathedral – would never be built, leaving the Memorial to the Missing of the Somme as his supreme creation. The completion of the Thiepval Memorial seems to have marked the end of a most productive phase in Lutyens's career, at a time when the architectural climate was changing dramatically. 'Here I am,' he concluded, writing from home in London, 'glad to be back – and a little sad that the graves work is closed as with Delhi, Spain, America all seem to close together – and now what will a new era bring?'

....

8

LEGACY

The unveiling of what was the last as well as the largest of the War Graves Commission's memorials was naturally reported in the daily press. *The Times* devoted a long pontifical editorial to musings on its significance: 'This is the shocked and troubled world's new conception of victory. We see victory now only as a great responsibility. [...] Let us remember with all our heart and soul, and make of these memorials beacons to light us through the darkest hours that may come.' But what seems extraordinary, and significant, is that the completion of a great work by the nation's most celebrated architect attracted virtually no critical comment. A new bank, a new block of flats or a speech by Lutyens was always reported in the architectural press, yet the unveiling of Thiepval was ignored by the *Architectural Review*, the *Architects' Journal* and the *Builder*, and even *Country Life* devoted but a paragraph to the event – and this without an accompanying photograph of the memorial. Only the *Architect & Building News* published a report by a 'special representative', who particularly admired 'the effect of the Stone of Remembrance, framed in the colossal arch, seen in silhouette against the sky beyond'. The completion of this huge structure on French soil also passed without comment by the French architectural press.

31. A strange tower standing in melancholy isolation: the Thiepval Memorial soon after completion.

It was as if everyone had now had enough of the war. The previous decade had been dominated by the war and the need to commemorate all those who never came home. But now five years had passed since the unveiling of the Menin Gate at Ypres and the mood of the nation as well as the architectural climate had somehow changed. R. C. Sherriff's play *Journey's End* was first performed in 1928 and this heralded a wave of memoirs and other publications which at last tried to tell what the Great War had actually been like. Before, those who had fought seemed to have been constrained, unable to convey to those who had stayed at home the horrors they had experienced. By 1932, however, the memoirs and novels of many writers who had been in the trenches had been published. *Undertones of War* by Edmund Blunden appeared in 1928, *Goodbye to All That* by Robert Graves in 1929 and *A Patriot's Progress* by Henry Williamson in 1930; Siegfried Sassoon's *Memoirs of a Fox-Hunting Man* and *Memoirs of an Infantry Officer* appeared in 1928 and 1930 respectively. Sassoon's war poetry was already in print and Wilfred Owen's work was at last published posthumously by Blunden in 1931. Then there was Erich Maria Remarque's *All Quiet on the Western Front*, which was published in both Germany and Britain in 1929, and was made into a film the following year. At last, the reality of the Great War as a monstrous, murderous tragedy was penetrating the public consciousness, fed hitherto on comfortable notions of British feats of arms and patriotism, and on stories of German atrocities that proved to be exaggerated if not mendacious. 'This book,' wrote Remarque, 'is to be neither an accusation nor a confession, and least of all an adventure, for death is not an adventure to those who stand face to face with it. It will simply tell of a generation of men who, even though they may have escaped its shells, were destroyed by the war.'

'War books suddenly came back into fashion in 1928–9,' Robert Graves later recalled: 'but to "debunk" rather than glorify.' The year 1928 also saw the death of the Earl Haig, which allowed his prodigal management of the military campaigns at last to be publicly questioned. Liddell Hart published his military history of the conflict, at first entitled *The Real War*, in 1930. In an epilogue to the 1934 edition, he noted the changing attitudes to the late war. The earlier anniversaries of the Armistice, he wrote, 'were dominated by two opposite emotions. On the one hand grief, a keener sense, now that the storm had passed, of the vacant places in our midst. On the other hand, triumph, flamboyant only in rare cases, but nevertheless a heightened sense of victory, that the enemy had been laid low. That mood again has passed. Armistice Day has become a commemoration instead of a celebration. [...] In this mood of reflection we are more ready to recognize both the achievements and the point of view of our late enemies, and perhaps all the more because we realize that both the causes and the course of war are determined by the folly and the frailty rather than by the deliberate evil of human nature. The war has become history, and can be viewed in the perspective of history. [...] for good or bad, it has shattered our faith in idols, our hero-worshipping belief that great men are different clay from common men. Leaders are still necessary, perhaps more necessary, but our awakened realization of their common humanity is a safeguard against either expecting from them or trusting in them too much.'

The changing mood was also caught by Ian Hay (Major John H. Beith) in his book about the Scottish National War

Memorial. 'At last came Victory, resounding and complete,' he recalled in 1931; 'exultation; and blind determination to make a hero of everybody who had contributed thereto. Then followed one vast reaction. Everybody announced that the War must now be forgotten. We had to get back to business. War books were unsaleable, War topics taboo. Having talked about nothing but the War for five years, we decided never to talk about it again. And now, twelve years later, we are talking about it more than ever. But the note is different. War has become a monstrous, unspeakable thing, and all the nations of Christendom are to-day combined in earnest, eager debate to drive it forever from among men.'

Against this background, the Memorial to the Missing of the Somme, if not seen as an indictment of the folly and callousness of certain great men, was perhaps an unwelcome tangible reminder of the pointless waste of life in the greatest disaster of British military history, and so it met with a thundering silence. Lutyens's memorial was not celebrated as there was nothing to celebrate, only much to mourn. At least, however, no Sassoon emerged to condemn it as a 'sepulchre of crime' or as a 'pile of peace-complacent stone': there was certainly no complacency about the Somme Memorial. But in a mood of tolerance tinged with cynicism – the climate of opinion which would lead to the desperate appeasement of Nazi Germany later in the decade – perhaps it had nothing new to say while being embarrassingly monumental. Nor could it be seen as a pacifist statement, although it certainly did not glorify war; designed, as it originally was, back in 1923, it spoke, rather, of an earlier ethos, of optimism, perhaps, and faith in the value of the sacrifice. A new generation, meanwhile, which was vaguely ashamed that it had been too young to fight – and which included Lutyens's admirers like Robert Byron and Christopher Hussey – simply did not wish to hear any more about the war, or any more justifications from the old men who had been responsible for the slaughter. Many preferred to look forward rather than back. Even so, it is hard to understand why even in *The Immortal Heritage*, Fabian Ware's own account of the work and policy of the Imperial War Graves Commission published in 1937, while there are photographs of the Menin Gate, Vimy Ridge, the Ulster Tower and many other memorials (including a perspective of Lutyens's as yet unfinished Australian memorial), there is no illustration depicting the sublime grandeur of the Thiepval arch.

Although cheap at the price (its estimated cost was £117,000, which worked out at £1 11s. 0d. per missing name compared with £1 16s. 0d. at the Menin Gate), Lutyens's memorial, unveiled during the economic difficulties of the Depression, may also have suffered from that narrow utilitarian tradition in Britain that considered that money was wasted on mere memorials and that it would have been better spent on practical things, that the dead were better remembered by useful structures for the living: village halls, hospitals and the like. The elderly Arts and Crafts architect W. R. Lethaby had complained in 1919 that 'the people asked for houses and we have given them stones'. However, with such buildings, the commemorative purpose is invariably soon forgotten after a few years. 'Does anyone say,' asked Sir Frederic Kenyon in a valedictory article published a week before the unveiling at Thiepval, 'as the Disciples of old, to what purpose is this waste, for the money might have been given to the poor? Not anyone who has seen the cemeteries and monuments. Not anyone who, in virtue of a dear life lost, has in these cemeteries or these battlefields some spot that is for ever England. Not anyone who thinks it worth while to spend the cost of a single day of war in paying our tribute to those who fell. Not anyone who sees in them a memorial of a great alliance, a reminder of the cost at which our country was kept free and great, and a pledge that, so far as in us lies, such sacrifices shall not again be required to preserve the liberties and the civilization of the world.' Alas, they soon would be.

Even so, perhaps it would have helped if the British government had been prepared to spend a little money on the living as well as on the dead. For his book on *The First Day on the Somme*, published in 1971, Martin Middlebrook interviewed men who had survived the carnage on 1 July 1916 and found that they were often still bitter at the way they had been treated after the war was over. For many – especially the maimed – their reward was unemployment and degradation. For one old soldier, there was 'One universal question which I have never seen answered: two or three million pounds a day for the 1914–18 war, yet no monies were forthcoming to put industry on its feet on our return from the war […]. I would lay puzzling why, why, after all we had gone through in the service of our country, we have to suffer such poverty, willing to work at anything but no work to be had.' And another said that 'Although I survived to reach the ripe old age of seventy-five, I look back, not with pride, but with disgust at the treatment meted out to the disabled ex-servicemen of my generation.' Some said that they would never fight for their country again.

After the unveiling, Thiepval was left to its few French inhabitants as well as to those who had survived the Somme and to the families of those who had not. No figures survive for the number of visitors who went to see the new Somme Memorial after it was unveiled, but visits to all the war cemeteries rose in the 1930s after a low point in 1926–7 (99,000 signed the visitors' books in the shelters in 1932 and 158,000 in 1938). A contemporary guide book to British memorials considered that 'When one has seen the Menin Gate, the Thiepval Memorial compels comparison and we realise that they are complementary; the Menin Gate is intimate and brings grief home to us. The massive Thiepval Memorial situated on a hill overlooking the valley of the Ancre with its history of carnage, emphasises the loneliness and solitude of death.' (Interestingly, the writer went on to observe that 'It is designed in the spirit of the twentieth century; no ornate decoration detracts from its purpose.') Visiting Thiepval was not always easy, however. The site of the memorial was more remote and isolated than the Menin Gate at Ypres, and not particularly welcoming. One former soldier wrote to the War Graves Commission in 1933 to complain that 'The so-called café which appears to be the only place of its kind in Thiepval is a disgrace and a scandal. Its proximity to the beautiful monument makes it the more odious. It is a large and squalid wooden hut whose only contents are a few greasy chairs and tables, half a dozen bottles (for no solid food appears obtainable), a party of disgusted visitors, and finally, millions of flies.' Perhaps that is why, later in the decade, another café was opened by a former despatch rider who also bought the grounds of the *château* and who would show visitors the dais used by the Prince of Wales and President Lebrun at the unveiling.

There was one last piece of unfinished business on the

Somme: the unveiling of Lutyens's long-delayed Australian National Memorial at Villers-Bretonneux, which took place in 1938. The following year a second World War began and its tower was damaged as yet again the German armies advanced through northern France in 1940, sweeping past Thiepval. For four years, this long-suffering part of France was again under German occupation. Thiepval was liberated by British forces on 3 September 1944. When the war ended the following year, the War Graves Commission had to start its work all over again as it was now facing the consequences of more battles and more casualties, in very different circumstances and in far-flung parts of Africa and Asia as well – although it was not until 1960 that its name was tactfully changed to the Commonwealth War Graves Commission.

There were also the consequences of delayed maintenance on and damage to its existing cemeteries and memorials to deal with. The Commission's staff reported on the state of affairs at Thiepval in February 1945. The Germans had almost always respected the British war cemeteries and memorials and 'The structure appears to be in sound condition.' The main problem with the memorial was the flaking of the brickwork. 'Water was dropping from the ceilings in many places, but it will be recalled that this has occurred ever since construction.' Indeed, one commentator at the unveiling thirteen years earlier had noticed that 'some panels appear already to be suffering from the extreme exposure of the site'. The Somme area is wet, and, as architects tend to forget, unheated structures deteriorate when left out in the rain. In short, the Thiepval Memorial was sodden, and this was partly Lutyens's fault. 'It would seem that the trouble is not wholly due to inferiority in the quality of the bricks (they are not engineering bricks) but to the fact that the disposal of the rain-water of the flats has been far from successful.' Not for the first time, Lutyens's artfully concealed down-pipes were causing problems.

A report carried out by the architect Austin Blomfield in 1949 confirmed this diagnosis: the lead flats on the roofs were simply too large for the down-pipes provided and 'the memorial is so exposed and gets so much rain that I doubt if, say, one sound pipe could deal with all four blocks, without overflooding'. But the French bricks, which were 'flaking to pieces', were also a problem, and 'the trouble is due to the brick makers not giving enough time to mixing and kneading the bricks before putting into moulds, but only pressing the earth into shape'. Blomfield considered the memorial to be dangerous and he recommended a complete refacing. This was carried out in 1952–5, when the internal drainage system was also improved.

More work was carried out in the 1960s when significant changes to the memorial were made, mostly unfortunate. Because the brickwork on the low forecourt walls continued to spall, it was proposed to rebuild them at a reduced height. The opinion was sought of Sir Edward Maufe, the architect of Guildford Cathedral, who had succeeded Kenyon as the Commission's Artistic Adviser and who had been appointed Principal Architect for the UK in 1944. In his report of 1961, Maufe wrote of Thiepval that 'one is again astounded by it; it appears to be Lutyens's greatest achievement; all the more it is necessary to improve its present unworthy surroundings'. This admiration did not, however, prevent Maufe from approving the modification of Lutyens's forecourt walls, an integral part of the overall conception. In consequence, the

32. An aerial view of Thiepval in the mid-1960s, after the forecourt walls had been lowered but before the walls enclosing the *rond point* were removed.

side walls were lowered in 1964 to a continuous low horizontal instead of gentle steps down from the basement level of the memorial – Lutyens was always concerned to express continuous horizontals – while the circular wall around the *rond point* was replaced partly by hedge and partly by a new curved seat where Lutyens had continued the principal axis towards the west. Given the supreme importance of the Thiepval Memorial today, these lost elements ought surely to be reinstated. Maufe also altered the surrounding planting, recommending *Cupressus Leylandii* on the avenues. The original planting plan (since apparently lost) had never been fully implemented as some of the chosen trees had failed to grow.

The one alteration to the memorial which, although large in scale, is defensible was the building of a monumental staircase from the eastern terrace down to the Anglo-French cemetery below. Before, any visitor to Thiepval – which by now often meant elderly veterans – had to return to the *rond point* from the memorial and then walk below the retaining walls to reach the cemetery. A design for a double-flight staircase, within brick walls maintaining the height of the podium, was prepared by Ralph Hobday, the Commission's senior architect. This was modified by Maufe, who wrote of the design in 1961 that 'It appears to me to work sweetly and is in the Lutyens manner, in no way detracting from the existing work.'

The brickwork continued to spall, however, owing to rain and frost. Siliconates were applied to reduce water penetration, but in vain. In 1970 it was reported that there was danger from falling brickwork and it was decided to reface the memorial for a second time. After tests, an English

Accrington 'Nori' sand-faced engineering brick was chosen. Work was under way in 1973, and this time the Commission was determined that the refacing would endure. Two inches was cut off the brick and concrete core to allow a cavity and a coating of asphalt behind the new brickwork, which was hung on bronze clamps. Unfortunately, the brickwork today does not look quite as Lutyens intended, in either colour or texture. Sir Peter Shepheard, who succeeded Lord Holford as the Commission's Artistic Adviser in 1975, later wrote about the refacing that 'I am still not convinced that this was right, but the project was nearly complete when I arrived on the scene.' What Shepheard did manage to do was to remove all the trees planted by Maufe and to restore the old planting, 'or one should say *absence* of planting'. This was because they obscured both battlefield views and most of the monument from a distance. (Today, however, the trees come so close to the memorial that it is difficult to appreciate the important diagonal views while, again, it is partly obscured from a distance.)

One major change has occurred at Thiepval since – one which would surely have surprised the founders of the War Graves Commission. This is the associated Visitor Centre, opened in 2004. The idea was promoted in 1998 to remedy the fact that there was nothing at Thiepval to explain to new generations of visitors what had happened in and around the place in 1916, nor were there any facilities or shelter at the site. Funds were raised independently by a committee chaired by Sir Frank Sanderson. The architects, chosen by competition, were French: PLAN 01, a group of four practices based in Paris, of whom the leading architects dealing with the Thiepval project were Nicolas Ziesel and Dominique Vity of KOZ Architectes. They produced a discreet, flat-roofed modern building sited between the memorial and Thiepval village, half sunk in the ground, partly of glass and partly faced with a sloping brick wall, which rightly makes no impact on the setting of Lutyens's monument. The visitor can now either go straight to the memorial or pass through this interesting and subtle building on the way, and inside a permanent exhibition tells the history of the war fairly and objectively.

The Thiepval Visitor Centre is a response to a phenomenon which was not envisaged forty years ago when, with the generation which fought in the Great War beginning to disappear, the Commonwealth War Graves Commission began to wonder if there would be any visitors to its cemeteries and memorials in the future. They need not have worried. Numbers have grown in recent years as interest in the war – encouraged by the popularity of family history – has, if anything, increased rather than diminished. Something like a quarter of a million people now visit Thiepval every year. Groups of schoolchildren regularly arrive, partly no doubt but not entirely in response to the history syllabus they are set, while the Great War and the Battle of the Somme continue to hold the imaginations of Britons born since the Second World War. 'Thiepval is one of life's finest classrooms,' as Michael Stedman puts it. In consequence, the Memorial to the Missing of the Somme now enjoys a greater stature and symbolic significance than probably at any time since it was unveiled. It also now seems abundantly clear that it is one of the finest creations of its prolific designer, Edwin Lutyens.

Nevertheless, the Thiepval Memorial matters because it is more than great architecture, a supreme monument. It speaks

33. One of the smallest arched tunnels at Thiepval, where the floor is given a distinctive pattern in brick and stone.

to us still because of the immense gravity of its purpose and because we – in Britain at least – remain haunted by the tragedy, futility and murderousness of the Battle of the Somme. Even with the help of all those names, it is still hard to grasp the fact that over eighty thousand men simply disappeared during that brutal campaign (for there are more names of the missing on the memorial at Pozières in addition to those at Thiepval), let alone that so many, many more died in it. A few of these names are famous – those of H. H. Munro, that is, the novelist 'Saki', and of the composer George Butterworth are carved on the walls at Thiepval – but the vast majority are not. As Martin Middlebrook wrote, the casualties were 'the unknown humble men, who never had a chance of becoming famous. They died in their thousands, those fine men of 1916. They died for love of country and 1s. a day. The soldiers of 1916 were not supermen; they did not belong to a special generation. They were merely ordinary Britons, who believed that they had to fight to save their country. It turned out that theirs was to be an unlucky and ill-used generation.' Thiepval can thus be seen not just as a memorial to the Missing of the Somme but to all the victims of the whole Great War; and even if that comprehension is confined to the Western Front, it means not just the British who suffered but the French as well, and not forgetting the former enemy, the Germans, many of whom still lie buried there – the bodies of seven more German soldiers were found when digging the foundations for the new Visitor Centre.

For the British, the experience of the Great War cannot be forgotten – even if the ubiquitous memorials could be wished away. It continues to interest, obsess and horrify. It also still generates debate and controversy. The 'lions led by donkeys' interpretation, exemplified by *Oh What a Lovely War!* – first put on stage by Joan Littlewood in 1963 and made into a film six years later – can be traced back to the war poets and novelists, to the first truthful depictions and debunkings of the red-tabbed officers in the late 1920s. But the Great War still cannot really be joked about as the suffering and the losses of 1914–18 remain too unbearably awful to contemplate. In the final series of the *Blackadder* television comedy, which was set in that war, the depiction of life in the trenches was essentially a satire on *Journey's End*, but even this comedy could only conclude with the comic characters going over the top to the sound of gunfire – and being killed, for we know that is how so many lives ended.

Some cannot bear revisionist interpretations and insist on maintaining that the men whose names are carved on the walls of Thiepval, and on the headstones in all the cemeteries on the Somme, died to some purpose. This was inevitable and understandable in the years immediately after the Armistice, but less comprehensible now. One of the least attractive aspects of the English is our refusal – manifest facts to the contrary – ever to admit we were wrong, or ever behaved in anything but an upright, heroic, honourable way, while former enemies are still demonised. So historians argue that the Great War really had to be fought because the wicked 'Huns' started it, and that the prodigal losses of the Somme and Passchendaele were somehow justified by a series of British tactical victories against an exhausted and starved German army in the latter months of 1918. This national self-justification even extends to trying to rehabilitate the repellent figure of Douglas Haig, although the motives for doing this must remain baffling. There is already a vast literature about the war and it continues to grow. What is depressing is that much of this is of the military trainspotting variety, as if recounting the minutiae of regimental deployments and the winning of medals somehow justifies the overall slaughter and the horrific conditions to which most soldiers were subjected. In such publications, the equal sufferings of the French, let alone of the Germans, are seldom much discussed, let alone such unpalatable facts as that men were often kept in the fight only by the threat from an officer's revolver or that, in the fury of battle, many surrendering prisoners were murdered – by both sides.

The Great War eventually changed Britain as it changed Europe, and led to social revolution. Knowing, as we do, how those regiments of volunteers were squandered; knowing, as we now do, that the British authorities were quite prepared to lose half a million men in the Somme campaign, and that they colluded with Douglas Haig after the war to falsify the record to try and protect his reputation, it is no longer possible to have so much trust in governments or military leaders. Nor, ultimately, is it possible to have total respect in the churches that were prepared to prostitute themselves to nationalist myths, although the sacrifice of young men between 1914 and 1918 can still have powerful meaning in sacramental terms today as it did for those who wanted the Christian Cross to rise over the dead. The veneer of civilisation is thin, and behind it there is always ruthlessness and brutality. The Great War continues to haunt us because it was the ultimate war; innocence really was destroyed, and we can only hope that we are never asked to undergo what the men of 1916 endured.

Although the past is a foreign country and it is often

foolish to interpret the behaviour of earlier generations by the standards and attitudes of today, it may well still seem shaming that one's own country was prepared to behave in, at best, such an incompetent or, worse, such a callous and ruthless manner towards its own citizens – and for such dubious motives. Even if the war had to be fought, and to the very end – a questionable proposition – it surely should have been fought efficiently. 'To throw good money after bad is foolish,' as Liddell Hart put it. 'But to throw away men's lives, where there is no reasonable chance of advantage, is criminal. [...] For such manslaughter, whether it springs from ignorance, a false conception of war or a want of moral courage, commanders should be held accountable to the nation.' The events of 1914–18 can seem the most important of any in the recent past; they still move, amaze, shock, horrify, infuriate, crush. It seems vitally necessary to identify with what those men experienced to make sense of what followed, and to understand Britain today. Comprehending the unspeakable brutality of the trenches requires an exercise of the imagination and can be a profoundly emotional experience, while visiting the cemeteries to gain a sense of the enormity of the organised brutality – and stupidity – of the Great War can be cathartic and redemptive.

Rising silently, magnificently above all this continuing controversy, the Memorial to the Missing of the Somme serves to remind us of our inescapable past. But some of the lessons it offers are difficult and painful. It is possible to have a sense that a huge, monstrous *crime* was committed, by the British as well as by other governments. Perhaps that is why the war continues to interest novelists as well as historians. There can be no better context for studying human courage, endurance and viciousness, and official callousness, cynicism and incompetence, than the Great War. The sheer vastness of the tragedy of the Somme and Passchendaele – to limit things again merely to the British experience – remains overwhelming and invites a passionate response. So, in the last few decades, there have been the novels of Pat Barker and Sebastian Faulks, revisiting the trenches yet again. Both were born after the Second World War yet, from childhood, were almost inexorably drawn to the events and myths of the First, like so many of their generation.

The Memorial to the Missing of the Somme makes an appearance in Faulks's *Birdsong*, published in 1993. 'Through the fields to her right Elizabeth saw a peculiar, ugly arch that sat among the crops and woods. She took it for a beet refinery at first, but then saw that it was too big: it was made of brick or stone on a monumental scale. It was as though the Pantheon or the Arc de Triomphe had been dumped in a meadow. [...] From near to, the scale of the arch became apparent: it was supported on four vast columns; it overpowered the open landscape. The size of it was compounded by its brutal modern design; although clearly a memorial, it reminded her of Albert Speer's buildings for the Third Reich.' It must be hoped that this aesthetic response to Lutyens's masterpiece is that of his modern character visiting Albert in 1978 rather than that of the novelist himself, for the facile identification of monumental Classical architecture with totalitarianism is as tired as it is ignorant. But never mind that there are no *columns* in the memorial, that there are sixteen piers, and that Elizabeth must have had very big ankles or was wearing very high heels, the memorial still has the effect intended.

'As she came up to the arch Elizabeth saw with a start that

it was written on. She went closer. She peered at the stone. There were names on it. Every grain of the surface had been carved with British names; their chiselled capitals rose from the level of her ankles to the height of the great arch itself; on every surface of every column as far as her eyes could see there were names teeming, reeling, over surfaces of yards, of hundreds of yards, over furlongs of stone. [...] "Who are these, these ...?" She gestured with her hand. "These?" The man with the brush sounded surprised. "The lost." "Men who died in this battle?" "No. The lost, the ones they did not find. The others are in the cemeteries." "These are just the ... unfound?" She looked at the vault above her head and then around in panic at the endless writing, as though the surface of the sky had been papered in footnotes. When she could speak again, she said, "From the whole war?" The man shook his head. "Just these fields."'

Even here, the Somme Memorial, rising above the trivial and quotidian, still speaks of great and terrible truths about the war, and about humanity. Perhaps the best interpretation of the continuing and compelling significance of the Great War to the British is Geoff Dyer's *The Missing of the Somme*, which appeared in 1994 and which ends with meditations at Thiepval. Dyer makes explicit what many of us vaguely sense when surrounded by those walls of names under Lutyens's high vaults. Noting that if, as it surely was, the twentieth century was one of departure, of migration, of exodus and of disappearance, 'then the Thiepval Memorial to the Missing casts a shadow into the future, a shadow which extends beyond the dead of the Holocaust, to the Gulag, to the "disappeared" of South America, and of Tiananmen'. To which litany we might now add Grozny, Iraq and Syria. 'That is why so much of the meaning of our century is concentrated here. Thiepval is not simply a site of commemoration but of prophesy, of birth as well as of death: a memorial to the future, to what the century had in store for those who were left, whom age would weary.' Thiepval is a universal monument, and, in that, it certainly is a modern Wonder of the World.

To see the Thiepval Memorial as representing the tragedy of the twentieth century should not encourage an idealised impression of a golden Edwardian Indian summer brought to a sudden end by the holocaust of 1914–18, for the pre-war world was far from placid, or just. It was an unstable and unpleasant society, and a potentially brutal one – as demonstrated by the behaviour of its ruling class afterwards, during the war. But there are alternative interpretations of the Great War that deserve consideration. One fact about those names lining the memorial is obvious but seldom commented on, which is that a good half of the British population was not represented among them; that is, the women. Some may have handed out white feathers during the war, but many women were nurses, or worked in factories or drove buses to sustain the nation's war effort. In consequence, after the war they were granted the beginnings of political and social equality. Whether they felt that emancipation was worth the sacrifice of fathers and sons, husbands, lovers and friends, it would now be presumptuous to speculate.

There are other positive aspects to the Thiepval Memorial, not least, the very fact that it was built and continues to exist. The government may indeed have fed millions into the industrialised slaughter with a callous indifference to the sanctity of human life when measured against the shifting aims of the war, but at least every life lost was commemorated by a headstone or by a name on a wall in a cemetery or on a memorial of conspicuous beauty and quality. As Ken Worpole writes at the end of his book on cemetery architecture, 'It should always be remembered that the last landscapes of human culture were also among the first. For it was when people began to mark the passage and place of death that they discovered their humanity.' And it is hugely cheering that these places in France, Belgium and elsewhere continue to be maintained with loving care by the Commonwealth War Graves Commission – funded by the governments of the British Commonwealth – long after the time when the generation that fought and died might have reached its natural three score years and ten and faded away peacefully. On one level, this care for foreign fields that are for ever England could be interpreted as a continuing assertion of former British power and prestige, but on another it is humane and civilised. Such places are important as tangible history, full of terrible lessons that we need to learn again and again, today as much as ever. And, just by existing, the Memorial to the Missing of the Somme testifies to the significance of 73,357 individual souls.

Perhaps what is most extraordinary is that, to commemorate a great tragedy, the defining experience of twentieth-century Britain, a designer was chosen who may have been tiresome, difficult, awkward and selfish but was nevertheless a transcendent genius of the highest order when it came to the handling of architectural form. Edwin Landseer Lutyens was, quite simply, the greatest of British architects, of any generation, and a man who, ultimately, lived only and cared only for his art; a man who believed that 'Architecture, with its love and passion, begins where function ends.' It was to this strange, complex artist to whom the nation turned, via Fabian Ware and his Imperial War Graves Commission, to memorialise the tragedy of the Somme. As with the Cenotaph, which, by some miracle, also came to him, he did not disappoint. After standing cogitating why and how the (temporary) Cenotaph was 'so noble a thing', J. M. Barrie had written to its creator with an explanation: 'It is how the war has moved you and lifted you above yourself.' The same was surely true of Thiepval.

The importance of the Somme Memorial, a century after the dreadful events it commemorates, is partly due to the revival of interest in Lutyens and his work as well as to the continuing British preoccupation with the events of 1914–18. Its present status is therefore partly a product of the changing fortunes of that dominant and ubiquitous twentieth-century tendency, the Modern Movement in architecture, as Lutyens's posthumous reputation suffered at first from denigration by modernists. When he died, there was no doubt of his pre-eminence, even if it was clear that the circumstances which gave rise to Lutyens's country houses, let alone New Delhi, would never return. Later, his work could be dismissed as irrelevant and his greatness was questioned. However, it is only since another World War that his astonishing achievement at Thiepval has been fully recognised.

Lutyens had spent the first few years of the Second World War with virtually no work and in declining health, coughing. He partly occupied himself, along with other Royal Academician architects, making a pompous and sterile plan for rebuilding London after the war. He died at home in Mansfield Street on New Year's Day 1944 at the age of seventy-four. His daughter Mary recalled how 'The news made little impact on me. The general horror of the war, the tragedies suffered by some of those very close to me and a bereavement of my own had left me numb at that time, but I wanted to get to Mother as quickly as possible. [...] Going up Whitehall, almost deserted, I quite unexpectedly found we were passing the Cenotaph. I was shattered. The aloof, lonely perfection of its beauty pierced me. [...] Returning [...] I passed the Cenotaph again. I can never pass it now without feeling he is there – it is his soul, the quintessence of his genius – as much a memorial to him as to the dead of two wars – but above all a triumphant affirmation of the spirit of harmony which makes order out of the chaos of materialism. Perfect order is perfect well-being.'

There was no doubt that Lutyens's death, five months before the Allied invasion of Normandy, marked the end of an era. 'Lutyens absent, the architectural scene is colder,' concluded one obituarist. 'A whole age has receded and its last monarch, Lutyens the magnificent, has resigned the sceptre.' 'He was a magician, a spell-binder, and few of us have not been in thrall to him,' wrote H. S. Goodhart-Rendel. 'He seems to leave behind him a grey world, full of grim architectural Puritans on the one hand and gentleman-like architects who do the done thing on the other.' His contemporary, ally and friend, Sir Fabian Ware, 'the great commemorator', followed him five years later, having resigned as Vice-Chairman of the Imperial War Graves Commission only in 1948.

With the Second World War at last over, it was time to look again at Lutyens's achievement in giving dignity to and memorialising the dead of the First now that yet more cemeteries and memorials were needed. The first writer really to praise the Somme Memorial in print was Arnold Whittick, who, in his book on *War Memorials* published in 1946, had no doubt of its supreme quality. 'It is a daring and imaginative conception which dominates the scene,' he wrote; 'and there is in this arch towering above the Somme battlefield an expression of aspiration associated with grandeur and power which, to those who have seen it, is an unforgettable spectacle. No memorial arch of the ancient or modern world has such a beauty of proportion or conveys in monumental form such an impression of inspired achievement. To me it is the finest architectural monument of the last war, and is a lasting testimony to the genius of its designer; while in the feelings and aspirations combined with mourning and sorrow that it conveys it is as impressive an architectural symbol as seems to be possible of the vast and melancholy human drama enacted on these battlefields.'

The studies and biography known as the *Lutyens Memorial* volumes were published in 1950 and, in his *Life of Sir Edwin Lutyens*, Hussey at last did justice to his hero's achievement on the Somme as he noted how 'his monumental work with the War Graves Commission produced a type of design in which classical notation was gradually reduced or eliminated, retaining the elements and proportions, to which he added subtleties of entasis, visual compensation, and curvature by means of a basically simple but complex geometry, that was likewise often implicit, not expressed. [...] His most complete extant monument in this key is the Thiepval Arch [...].' Hussey described this manner as Lutyens's Elemental Mode, in which 'he carried the art of architecture into a realm unvisited by any save its supreme exponents'. 'There is sublimity in this great abstraction of pure architecture,' he wrote of Thiepval. 'To the emotional mind, its multitude of arches may represent portals to the four quarters of the wide horizon, ever open for the spirits of the lost. That imaginative aspect is of the kind that may well have been in the Architect's mind, as certainly were its visual qualities of mystery, of texture, and of deep shadows. But it was axiomatic of his Elemental Mode of design that the motivations of heart and eye must be subordinated to and disciplined by the mind; their promptings be the effects of certain forms combined in some ratio or science that is for the architect to ascertain, leaving nothing to chance.'

Hussey was insistent that, in his late work, Lutyens had left behind a vital legacy. He concluded his *Life* by writing that 'We can now [...] recognise that the Thiepval Memorial, the Poultry bank, and the designs for Liverpool Cathedral [...] constitute forward bases, of great cogency, established by Lutyens's genius as starting points for the advance of the Humanist tradition into the questionable future. They embody in architectural language his "true spirit", his faith in accumulated knowledge, his insistence on unity based on reality, and his humanity.' But that future was indeed questionable, and the 'Humanism' of Lutyens's generation was being supplanted by the mechanistic functionalism of the ascendant modernists, those 'grim architectural Puritans'. By the end of the 1950s, the work of Lutyens seemed an embarrassing irrelevance, fatally associated with past Imperial ambitions and the smug, sybaritic Edwardians.

The lowest point for Lutyens's reputation was probably his centenary in 1969, when funds could not be raised to mount an exhibition at the Royal Academy and the *RIBA Journal* gave space to the modernist architects Alison and Peter Smithson to argue that Lutyens had perverted the course of modern English architecture. The previous year, however, the disastrous gas explosion at Ronan Point, a block of prefabricated concrete council flats in East London, had stimulated the process of questioning the ideals and assumptions of the 'Modern Movement'; a reaction which would eventually lead to Post-Modernism, the New Vernacular and the present more tolerant eclecticism. In comparison with the formal aridity and functional shortcomings of the new concrete and glass architecture which was overwhelming every city in Britain in the 1960s, Lutyens's work now seemed full of richness, subtlety and meaning. The formality and ambiguity of Lutyens's architecture was already being defended by the American architect Robert Venturi and by Allan Greenberg, a South African, and in the 1970s interest in it grew. In 1972 another American, the historian David Gebhard, could write of Viceroy's House that it 'stands as a formidable argument: an argument for classical humanism, for man's ability to control and at the same time to accommodate himself to his physical and social environment – and against those planners and architects who, as ageing period pieces, still cling to the tenets of the "Modern Movement" in architecture'.

One inspired advocate of Lutyens was the English architect Roderick Gradidge, who, in an essay on 'Edwin Lutyens: The Last High Victorian' published in 1976, gave a brilliant analysis of the design for Thiepval. Gradidge took a very unfashionable line by arguing that Lutyens's remarkable grasp of three-dimensional form and his ability to integrate planes and recessions on different elevations had nothing to do with his adoption of Classicism but derived from High Victorian Gothic and the work of church architects like G. E. Street.

'Most buildings from outside seem to impinge on space and from the inside to enclose space,' he argued, 'but at Thiepval, because of the relationship of the arches in three dimensions, space seems to flow through and around the building with a special rhythm which is given a further *rubato* by the relationship of wall planes, sometimes setting back on one elevation, sometimes on the other, but rarely on both elevations at the same time – a trick incidentally also used by Lutyens to great effect on the Cenotaph. The result is that the mind has difficulty in deciding exactly what type of building Thiepval really is. The triumphal arch becomes a memorial cenotaph in one view, in another it is a solid memorial tower, its base pierced by arches in all directions. In fact it is all these forms, all interlocked in one building. For the first time in two thousand years an architect has found something new to do with the triumphal arch, and he was in a position to do this because he was brought up within the tradition of the Gothic Revival with a Gothic Revival sense of form.'

In 1977 an exhibition of the memorial and cemetery architecture of the Great War called *Silent Cities* was held in the Heinz Gallery of the Royal Institute of British Architects and it was dominated by a huge photograph of the Thiepval arch. Four years after this, the large and comprehensive exhibition that Lutyens deserved was mounted by the Arts Council of Great Britain at the Hayward Gallery in London. Designed by Piers Gough, the final room contained the model of Lutyens's unbuilt Cathedral that had been first exhibited at the Royal Academy in 1934 next to a large new model of the Memorial to the Missing of the Somme, made semi-transparent to reveal the nature of its geometry. It was in the catalogue accompanying this exhibition that Sir John

Summerson first published his essay on 'Arches of Triumph: The Design for Liverpool Cathedral' in which he analysed that most complex and resonant conception in terms of the Roman triumphal arch as well as of the legacy of the Renaissance. Thiepval, 'the greatest of all Lutyens's memorials in size and the most liberated in form', naturally came into the story, and Summerson described how, in the Memorial, 'The Roman model is ruthlessly stripped, dissected and rebuilt, its massive shoulders cut away and their weight piled on top of the centre arch. Then, beneath the springing of this arch, the whole monument reproduces itself. It does so twice. Each of the lateral arches becomes the centre arch of a secondary monument, reproducing in its smaller arches the proportions of those of the first. The three monuments interlock with an appearance of innocent simplicity. In this interlocking the premises of the Liverpool design are, for the first time stated.'

Since the Lutyens exhibition of 1981–2, his stature is assured, and there is now a new and growing literature on his work, not least on the war cemeteries and memorials. Nor is this appreciation confined to Britain; in 2000, the Italian journal *Casabella* carried an article by Sissi Castellano on Lutyens's war cemeteries in northern France accompanied by superbly illustrated studies of Thiepval, Arras, Villers-Bretonneux, Etaples and other cemeteries. Seeing Lutyens as representative of a richer modern tradition in the twentieth century than that isolated by historians of the Modern Movement, Castellano insisted that 'It is precisely in these works that we can fully grasp the timelessness of the architecture of Lutyens. A timelessness that is evident not only in its capacity to investigate a possible synthesis between different cultures, by also in its ability to find an autonomous, original way to express modernity within an established tradition.' Ten years later, inspired by this article, the Dutch architect Jeroen Geurst published an impressive detailed study of all of Lutyens's war cemeteries and associated memorials in France and Belgium, analysing their plans and his ability 'to achieve countless variations with a limited number of resources, without resorting to repetition ... The cemeteries, besides being places for contemplation, turn out to be pages from a textbook for architects that is universally applicable.'

Nor is there any doubt today that the Thiepval Memorial is one of Lutyens's finest creations, but its pre-eminence is in part the result of its plangent significance in representing a central, defining event in modern British history, a disaster that cast its shadow over the remainder of the century – and beyond. In the cause of historical objectivity, it is therefore important not to read into the memorial more than Lutyens and the War Graves Commission intended. There is certainly no triumph, no victory in the Thiepval arch, although there is no humility either; it does not glorify war, but dignifies the wasteful sacrifice of young men by remembering them in a stupendous, breathtaking architectural gesture. War may be an evil, and the Great War a particular tragedy, but Lutyens's arch, rooted as it is in tradition while being at once entirely novel, is not a pacifist statement. It invites contemplation, but although it is assertive and proud, it does not hector.

The danger of an over-emotional interpretation of the memorial is exemplified by an essay by the American architectural historian Vincent Scully on 'Palladio, the English Garden, and the Modern Age', published in 1991. Thiepval was here described partly as a prelude to a discussion of the still-controversial Vietnam War Memorial in Washington, DC, designed by Maya Lin, a minimalist design which adopted the device of covering walls with intimidating lists of names of the dead as used long before by the Imperial War Graves Commission (with rather better lettering). 'Lutyens's Thiepval menaces the living, ferociously guards the dead. But in Maya Lin's memorial the ground opens for us all.' Scully insisted that Thiepval helps us perceive 'the evil, empty face of war'. It is 'an enormous monster; its tondi are eyes; its high arch screams. It is the open mouth of death, the ultimate "portrait" of landscape art that rises up to consume us all. The monster stands behind an aspect of grass. There is no path for us. We must violate the grass. Closer, we are enveloped by the creature's great gorge. One sarcophagus like a palate lies within it, under the arch.'

While it is hard to imagine any visitor to Thiepval not being profoundly moved by the resonant melancholy power of the architecture, Scully's reaction is merely histrionic. 'It should be said that everybody who visits the monument is weeping by now. It is this that does it: the terrible courage of human beings advancing in the open towards the monster, who is absolute – absolute pain and nothingness,' he continued (possibly, but possibly not, referring to the headstones in the cemetery below). 'He is emptiness, meaninglessness, insatiable war and death. There is no victory for the dead. All that courage wasted. But there they stand, the men, unbroken. It is not to be borne.' An anthropomorphic interpretation of architecture may sometimes have purpose, but to regard Lutyens's sophisticated and restrained distillation of the Classical tradition as an intimidating, monstrous metaphor for war is surely as absurd as it is blinkered.

No matter; like all great buildings, the Somme Memorial rises high above its critics. Is a work of architecture of its time, yet its emotional power seems timeless. Thiepval could only have been designed when it was; it is a product of a rare period of grand sophistication in British architecture. It must be hoped that such a monument may never be required again, but if it was, nothing commensurate with that hollow arched pyramidal pylon could ever now be achieved. That the Thiepval arch, like the Cenotaph and other memorials, continues to move and to awe testifies to the enduring resonance and comprehensibility of the Classical tradition, but few but Lutyens could ever handle that language of form with such precision and true originality. The Memorial to the Missing of the Somme, indeed, was precisely the commission to exploit that rare combination of mathematical science and intuitive emotional power that Lutyens's later work manifests. As he maintained, 'Everything should have an air of inevitability' and it is impossible to imagine the Thiepval Memorial being different in any way. It is the absolute, ultimate pure monument – but one with terrible meaning. It also stands as a reproach to the aridity of so much of the architecture of the Modern Movement which challenged Lutyens's 'Humanism' as well as exposing the amateurish mediocrity of so much modern Classicism today.

It is also extraordinary, perhaps, that what can be regarded as the greatest executed British work of monumental architecture of the twentieth century – 'building' will not do as a pure monument need not meet the functional demands of human existence – should stand across the English Channel, in a foreign country, in France. But that, in itself, emphasises that though Britain may once have had an Empire (whose dead also lie densely in France and Belgium), we are inextricably and gloriously part of Continental Europe. The only pity is that more do not know Thiepval, for there stands a monument of central importance in Britain's history that is of the greatest intellectual complexity and emotional power – and of supreme originality – which, by its sublime massing and poignant openness, directly conveys a sense of the eternally tragic.

34. Lest We Forget: Thiepval soon after Armistice Day in 2005.

AFTERWORD

It is now a decade since this book was first published. In that time, the Memorial to the Missing of the Somme has become even better known, increasingly used on television and in newspapers as a recognisable image to symbolise the death and loss of the Great War. Visitor numbers at Thiepval have continued to increase, although, of all the cemeteries and memorials maintained by the Commonwealth War Graves Commission, it is still the Menin Gate at Ypres which is best known and nearby Tyne Cot which attracts the most visitors.

Attitudes to these things have certainly changed since I first saw the Thiepval Arch forty years ago in the company of John Harris when we were conducting research for the pioneering *Silent Cities* exhibition mounted in London in 1977. At that time there were comparatively few visitors, while the Commonwealth War Graves Commission itself then seemed, if not moribund, then rather tired and intro- verted. The Commission had recently moved its offices from central London to Maidenhead, most unfortunately discard- ing some of its archives in the process, and the assumption seemed to be that once the First World War generation had died out, there would be little public interest in the cemeteries and monuments in its care and so they had no long term future. This could scarcely have been more wrong.

Today there is great interest in war memorials and cemeteries: both in what they are and represent but also in their design and artistic merit. The War Memorials Trust, founded in 1997, actively encourages the restoration of the estimated 100,000 war memorials in the United Kingdom and compiles an online survey of their location and condition. Historic England (formerly English Heritage) has been anxious to add many of them to the statutory list of structures of historical and architectural interest while offering grants towards their repair. Even the British government has taken more interest. As part of its contribution to marking the anniversaries of significant events of 1914–1918, the Chancellor of the Exchequer announced, in his 2014 Autumn statement, that £1.6 million had been allotted for 'restoration and enhancement' work on the memorial at Thiepval in anticipation of the centenary of the Battle of the Somme (we must hope that some of this may be spent on reinstating the low walls designed by Lutyens in front of the memorial which were foolishly removed in the 1960s).

There has certainly been increasing appreciation of the value of the noble work of the CWGC and more interest in its foundation and history, while the Commission itself has become more responsible and responsive, much more conscious of the historical and artistic importance of the monuments it maintains. The colossal achievement of its founder, Sir Fabian Ware, has at last secured wider recognition, what with the broadcast of Stephen Wyatt's 2007 award-winning radio play about him, *Memorials to the Missing*, and the publication in 2013 of David Crane's superb biography, *Empires of the Dead*. In September 2014, an English Heritage 'Blue Plaque' was unveiled on Ware's former home in Wyndham Place, Marylebone, an accolade proposed by Stephen Wyatt.

Much of this activity was, of course, encouraged by the approach of the centenary of the outbreak of the First World War. This, for some, has not been entirely welcome, for, since August 2014, it can be depressing constantly to be reminded of events largely categorised by failure and massive loss of life through the gloomy litany of anniversaries: Mons, First Ypres, Neuve-Chapelle, Gallipoli, Loos ... Furthermore, connected with remembrance in recent years has been the growth of a culture of what might be called insular jingoism, if not militarism. There has been a certain 'deification of the military' actively promoted by governments in recent years (it is surely significant that having what is now called Armed Forces Day was first promoted by the Chancellor of the Exchequer in 2006), very possibly to justify and cover up for Britain's dubious and disastrous military involvement in Iraq, Afghanistan and elsewhere – modern neo-imperialist adventures also characterised by the incompetence and official cynicism which can be seen in the official conduct of the First World War.

Recent historical writing has sought to try and understand the circumstances which lead to the outbreak of a war so devastating that it almost destroyed European civilisation. The magisterial books by Christopher Clark and Margaret MacMillan suggest that the catastrophe of 1914 was caused, in part, by secret treaties, devious and incompetent diplomacy together with imperialist ambitions and a culture of militarism from which Great Britain cannot be exculpated. But this research has made little impact on the British popular understanding of the First World War. There still seems to be the need to see Germany as the villain and Britain's role as entirely honourable. Clearly Imperial Germany must take much of the blame for what happened after the assassination at Sarajevo, but so must Serbia, Russia and not least Italy, while Great Britain was not entirely innocent. This tendency to see Britain as always in the right in that brutal, stupid war now even extends to rehabilitating the reputation of the dreadful Douglas Haig (how many know that the Commander-in-Chief who orchestrated the Allied victory on the Western Front in 1918 was in fact French: Ferdinand Foch?). Surely, after a century, it is time to stop the blame game and indulging in smug national superiority. Indeed, perhaps the best way to approach what happened between 1914 and 1918, at least in Europe, is to understand it as an interminable orgy of madness and wickedness. Which is why the war should continue to be studied, and remembered.

One product of this culture, of Britain's continuing obsession with and self-justifying narrative about both twentieth-century world wars (which baffles and dismays many sympathetic foreigners), has been the extraordinary proliferation, particularly in London, of yet more new war memorials, dedicated to particular campaigns or aspects of the conflicts. Most of these are of little or no artistic merit. The better examples, architecturally, such as the Commonwealth Gates at the top of Constitution Hill, look to the work of the architects of the Imperial War Graves Commission for inspiration. Others exploit and vulgarise that tradition, such as the overweening Bomber Command Memorial near Hyde Park Corner, which is far too large and distressingly triumphalist in tone, as well as architecturally pedestrian. But the main objection to many of these new memorials is that they are essentially superfluous: in London the Cenotaph says it all.

Of course war, loss and sacrifice should be remembered, if only as an object lesson – that is why the war cemeteries are maintained by the CWGC and Lutyens' great arch stands near the Somme at Thiepval. But what is distressing today is our insularity in remembrance, as if Britain (even England) was the only nation involved, the only nation that suffered. Little heed is paid to the losses of our allies, let alone any sympathy for the sufferings of our former enemies a century ago. Such insular jingoism was evident in the huge popular success of the centenary memorial installation at the Tower of London in 2014 by Paul Cummins and Tom Piper entitled *Blood Swept Lands and Seas of Red*. It was an imaginative and appropriate idea to fill the Tower's moat with a vast sea of red ceramic poppies, emphasising the scale of the British death toll during the Great War, but much stress was laid on the exact number of them: 888,246. This figure is a little puzzling. It is closest to the CWGC's estimate of deaths for Britain and its Colonies, which is 887,711 and therefore excludes the Australians, New Zealanders, Canadians, South Africans, Indians and other parts of the British Empire who all came to Britain's aid. The red poppies memorial therefore unwittingly betrayed Fabian Ware's inclusive Imperial vision in memorialisation.

It is in fact possible, after a century, to be more eirenic and less exclusive, understanding 1914–1918 as a European catastrophe, a European civil war as well as a total, *world* war. In France, a new and rather different International Memorial was unveiled in November 2014 at the vast national necropolis at Notre-Dame de Lorette near Arras. It is a huge open elliptical ring, 129 metres long and 75 wide, constructed of steel fibre and designed by Philippe Prost. It demonstrates that a modernist aesthetic can in fact work for memorials and it succeeds in being monumental, without sentimentality or vulgarity or, most importantly, triumphalism. The structure's purpose is revealed on the promenade on the inner side of the ring, almost a quarter of a mile long, where, on angled panels like the pages of books, are inscribed some 580,000 names. These are of young men who died in Artois and French Flanders in the Great War and they include *everyone*, friend and foe alike, listed in alphabetical order – French, German, Canadian, Indian, Australian, British, even Czechs, Slovaks and others – regardless of nationality, rank, race or religion. As the official press release put it, the new memorial 'falls within a more general reflection which does not celebrate the claimed victory of some or stigmatise those who were defeated. Instead it focuses on the shared suffering that was experienced by all soldiers, the mass death which characterised the wars of the industrial era …' It is cheering that such generosity of spirit and absence of nationalism is now possible, despite the fact that France's casualties in the Great War – almost 1.4 million – were many more than those of the British Empire. In this context, it is a mercy to recall that the Memorial to the Missing of the Somme proudly bears the dedication 'AUX ARMEES FRANCAISE ET BRITANNIQUE …'

Remembering inevitably evokes the future. How long can the governments of Britain and the other contributors to the CWGC annual budget go on justifying the expense of maintaining those many hundreds of cemeteries and memorials, so resisting the inevitable effects of time? Surely interest in the physical legacy of the Great War and the need to preserve

35. Reconciliation rather than triumph and focusing on the
shared suffering experienced by all soldiers: the new International
Memorial at Notre-Dame de Lorette near Arras designed
by Philippe Prost and unveiled in November 2014.

it must eventually wane as more generations pass on. Distant events will lose their impact and significance; national myths and patriotic emotions may fade away, as they long have with Agincourt. Although, after two centuries, the victory at Waterloo continues to resonate in Britain (partly because the bicentenary fell in 2015), the name for most people is now that of a railway station rather than a battle, and the memory of quarter-century long struggle with Revolutionary and Napoleonic France is no longer immediate, no longer necessary to national identity. Similarly, the tragedy and loss of the Great War must surely eventually recede from popular consciousness.

The Memorial to the Missing of the Somme at Thiepval, with its vast planes of brickwork and problematic flat roofs, will continue to require annual maintenance. But if that ever ceases, if it is ever abandoned, something substantial and astonishing will survive. Wind and rain may eventually efface the explanatory inscriptions and those vast walls of names, so making its meaning obscure as a monument to unimaginable loss, to the self-sacrifice, heroism, folly and murderousness of human beings. The name of Edwin Lutyens may become as recondite as those of Henry Yevele, Anthemius of Tralles or Iktinos. But as long as monumental masonry – brick and stone – stands, despite the ravages of time and nature, this extraordinary, sublime structure will continue to awe the visitor, proclaiming human genius in the organisation of three-dimensional form and mass, and the power of pure architecture to convey feeling and emotion.

Gavin Stamp
November 2015

MAKING A VISIT?

Thiepval is some six kilometres to the north-east of Albert in the *département* of Somme. It lies on the left bank of the Ancre where the D151 road from Aveluy to Grandcourt crosses the D73 from Pozières to Auchonvillers. The new Visitor Centre is open all day all the year round. Thanks to the advent of the Eurostar, it is now possible to travel from London to Thiepval and back in a day by taking an early train to Lille. A short walk (down the Avenue Le Corbusier) from Lille Europe reaches the old station, now called Lille Flandres, from which trains go to Amiens via Douai, Arras and Albert. The last part of the railway journey down the Ancre valley affords the view of the Memorial to the Missing which Lutyens intended, with the great arch and tower seen on axis at the top of the hill. From Albert, Thiepval is a short taxi ride away.

It is, however, well worth making a longer visit as there is so much more to see in and around Albert to do with the Great War. There are, of course, the many British war cemeteries concentrated in the area of the Somme offensive, and the Commonwealth War Graves Commission issues the standard Michelin 1:200,000 maps overprinted with a terrifying number of purple dots indicating their locations, together with a key. A little to the north-west of Thiepval is Connaught Cemetery (by Reginald Blomfield, G. H.

Goldsmith, Assistant Architect), with 1,278 burials – mostly of Ulstermen who attacked the Schwaben Redoubt on 1 July 1916. Bodies from nine nearby burial grounds were reinterred here. Close by is Mill Road Cemetery (by Herbert Baker, A. J. S. Hutton, Assistant Architect), with 1,298 burials. To the south of Thiepval, nearer Authuille and close to where the Leipzig Redoubt stood, is Blighty Valley Cemetery in Authuille Wood (by Baker and Hutton), with 993 burials, and Lonsdale Cemetery (by Baker and Hutton), with 1,521 burials. But there are many more British cemeteries nearby, too numerous to list here, but all indicated by the special signposts of the CWGC.

The French and German war cemeteries are less scattered and much more concentrated. Just outside Albert to the east, on the road to Fricourt, is one of the French Nécropoles Nationales, created in 1923 and containing 6,290 graves and with 2,879 casualties, mostly from 1916, in a mass grave. At Fricourt is the Deutsche Soldatenfriedhof or German war cemetery, created by the French in 1920 and taken over by the Volksbund Deutsche Kriegsgräberfürsorge in 1929; some 17,000 casualties of the Battle of the Somme lie buried here, with 11,970 of them in a mass grave (Manfred von Richtofen, the "Red Baron', was buried here for a time before his body was taken back to Germany). A little to the south of the German cemetery is the (British) Fricourt New Military Cemetery, designed by A. J. S. Hutton, a particularly beautiful and poignant walled enclosure in the middle of a field, with only 210 burials.

Then there are the memorials. Regimental and other memorials are scattered all over the Somme battlefield, but the most notable monuments near Thiepval are the Ulster

Tower, the replica of Helen's Tower at Clandeboye which is the 36th Ulster Division memorial, and the Memorial to the Missing of the Fifth Army, which is part of Pozières British Cemetery to the south-west of Thiepval. Designed by W. H. Cowlishaw, this records the names of 14,690 more missing of the Somme campaigns (many of them killed in 1918). Further to the west, outside Longueval, is the South African National Memorial designed by Sir Herbert Baker, in Delville Wood. A separate museum opened here in 1986.

As regards Edwin Lutyens, his other significant works for the IWGC are further afield, notably the Australian National War Memorial in the British Military Cemetery at Villers-Bretonneux and the Memorial to the Missing in the Faubourg d'Amiens Cemetery at Arras. Cemeteries in the Somme area for which Lutyens was Principal Architect are: Albert Communal Cemetery Extension; Assevillers New British Cemetery; Beacon Cemetery, Sailly-Laurette; Bronfay Farm Military Cemetery, Bray-sur-Somme; Cerisy-Gailly MC; Citadel New MC, Fricourt; Daours CCE; Dive Copse BC, Sailly-le-Sec; Gézaincourt CCE; Grove Town C., Méaulte; Hamel MC, Beaumont-Hamel; Hangard CCE; Heilly Station C., Méricourt l'Abbé; Hem Farm MC, Hem-Monacu; La Neuville BC, Corbie; Méaulte MC; Méricourt l'Abbé CCE; Puchevillers BC; Rosières-en-Santerre CCE; Ste Emilie Valley C., Villers-Faucon; Serre Road No. 2 Cemetery; and Villers-Bocage CCE. All these cemeteries and more are illustrated, discussed and analysed in Tim Skelton & Gerald Gliddon, *Lutyens and the Great War* (Frances Lincoln, London, 2008) and Jeroen Geurst, *Cemeteries of the Great War by Sir Edwin Lutyens* (010 Publishers, Rotterdam, 2010).

There are several published guides which deal with the

memorials and cemeteries as well as the military history of the First World War battlefields and of the Somme area in particular. These include Rose E. B. Coombs, *Before Endeavours Fade* (After the Battle, London, 1983); Martin and Mary Middlebrook, *The Somme Battlefields: A Comprehensive Guide from Crécy to the Two World Wars* (Viking, London, 1991); Tonie and Valmai Holt, *Battlefields of the First World War: A Traveller's Guide* (Pavilion Books, London, 1993); Paul Reed, *Battleground Europe. Walking the Somme: A Walker's Guide to the 1916 Somme Battlefield* (Leo Cooper, London, 1997); and, especially, Michael Stedman, *Battleground Europe. Somme: Thiepval* (Leo Cooper, London, 1995). An illustrated survey of military cemeteries in Europe – of all nationalities – is provided by Peter and Marco on the website www.unfortunate-region.org. Much to be recommended is Michael Barker and Paul Atterbury, *The North of France: A Guide to the Art, Architecture, Landscape and Atmosphere of Artois, Picardy and Flanders* (Heyford Press, London, 1990). This deals, amongst much else, with the buildings of Albert which rose again in the 1920s and which should not be missed: in particular the Church of Notre-Dame-de-Brebières, the Hôtel de Ville and the railway station.

Finally, the Historial de la Grande Guerre at Péronne must be mentioned. It is a remarkable new museum and archive (designed by Henri Ciriani) which opened in 1992 and that aims to go beyond conventional military history to present a picture of the war in a wider context and from the points of view of France, Britain and Germany.

FURTHER READING

THE BATTLE OF THE SOMME

There is such a depressingly huge literature on the Great War that it is difficult to know where to begin. For this book, I consulted Liddell Hart's pioneeringly revisionist *A History of the World War 1914–1918* (Faber and Faber, London, 1934), originally published as *The Real War* (1930), as well as A. J. P. Taylor, *The First World War: An Illustrated History* (Hamish Hamilton, London, 1963); John Terraine, *The First World War 1914–1918* (Hutchinson, London, 1965); Denis Winter, *Haig's Command: A Reassessment* (Viking, London, 1991); John Keegan, *The First World War* (Hutchinson, London, 1998); Niall Ferguson, *The Pity of War* (Allen Lane, London, 1998); and Michael Howard, *The First World War* (Oxford University Press, London, 2002). A good summary of the war and its aftermath is provided by the illustrated *Thiepval Exhibition Centre Guidebook* (2004). It will be evident that I am more sympathetic to accounts of the war that question its motives and conduct rather than those that merely catalogue and vaunt feats of arms.

As regards the Somme campaign in particular, I consulted John Harris, *The Somme: Death of a Generation* (Zenith, London, 1966); Martin Middlebrook, *The First Day on the Somme, 1 July 1916* (Allen Lane, London, 1971);

Lyn Macdonald, *Somme* (Michael Joseph, London, 1983); and John Keegan, *The Face of Battle: A Study of Agincourt, Waterloo and the Somme* (Jonathan Cape, London, 1976 and Barrie and Jenkins, London, 1988) – all of which deal with the experiences of the individual soldier as well as with Haig's grand plans. The more general histories of the First World War naturally tend to deal with strategic objectives and military dispositions. For the actual conditions that men endured, for descriptions of the squalid, brutal and highly dangerous circumstances in which men fought and died, the memoirs of survivors remain essential. Such famous texts as Edmund Blunden's *Undertones of War* (1928), Charles Edmonds's *A Subaltern's War* (1929), Robert Graves's *Goodbye to All That* (1929), Henry Williamson's *The Patriot's Progress* (1930) and, on the other side, Ernst Jünger's *Storm of Steel* (1920; English translation Allen Lane, 2003) all deal with the Somme battles, although none of these authors was in the front line on 1 July. For the experience of going over the top that day, see F. P. Crozier, *A Brass Hat in No Man's Land* (Jonathan Cape, London, 1930) and illuminating insights into the conduct of the Somme campaign are provided by Lieut.-Col. C. O. Head in *The Art of Generalship* (Aldershot, n.d., *c.* 1930). A revealing discussion of these literary sources is given in Paul Fussell, *The Great War and Modern Memory* (Oxford University Press, New York and London, 1975).

WAR MEMORIALS

The twentieth century generated more, and larger, war memorials than ever before, but remarkably little has been written about them – at least in English. The First World

War stimulated several historical studies to provide precedents, such as Lawrence Weaver's *Memorials and Monuments* (Country Life, London, 1915), but there have been few general histories since. The principal works are Arnold Whittick, *War Memorials* (Country Life, London, 1946) and Alan Borg, *War Memorials: From Antiquity to the Present* (Leo Cooper, London, 1991). The subject of war memorials and cemeteries is also discussed in James Stevens Curl, *A Celebration of Death* (Constable, London, 1980), while some early memorials are mentioned in Howard Colvin, *Architecture and the After-Life* (Yale University Press, New Haven and London, 1991). There is a considerable literature on the history of cemeteries but far less on memorials, particularly recent memorials. Part of the problem is, as Edwin Heathcote writes in *Monument Builders: Modern Architecture and Death* (Academy Editions, Chichester, 1999), 'the subject of death in modern architecture has been largely avoided'. The subject is, however, touched on by Ken Worpole in his *Last Landscapes: The Architecture of the Cemetery in the West* (Reaktion, London, 2003).

Memorials of the First World War are discussed in Jay Winter, *Sites of Memory, Sites of Mourning: The Great War in European Cultural History* (Cambridge University Press, Cambridge, 1995), and by Alex King in *Memorials of the Great War in Britain: The Symbolism and Politics of Remembrance* (Berg, Oxford, 1998). A melancholy catalogue is provided by C. F. Cernot, *British Public Schools War Memorials* (Roberts and Newton, London, 1927), and a wider survey is provided by Derek Boorman, *At the Going Down of the Sun: British First World War Memorials* (William Sessions, York, 1988), and the same author's *For Your Tomorrow* (Derek Boorman,

York, 1995) does the same for British Second World War Memorials. A comprehensive survey, full of information, has recently been provided by Mark Quinlan, *British War Memorials* (Authors On Line, Hertford, 2005). That several of these books are privately published suggests a reluctance by established publishers to tackle the subject. An interesting if abstruse illustrated French survey of First World War memorials is provided by J.-M. de Busscher, *Les Folies de l'industrie* (Archives d'Architecture Moderne, Brussels, 1981), while John Garfield records with his fine photographs graves of all nationalities – not just on the Western front but in Italy, Macedonia and Gallipoli – in his *The Fallen: A Photographic Journey through the War Cemeteries and Memorials of the Great War, 1914–18* (Leo Cooper, London, 1990); second edition, Spellmount, Stroud, 2014.

THE ARCHITECT

The architecture of Sir Edwin Lutyens has inspired a very distinguished and considerable literature, even if nowhere near as large as that devoted to his contemporaries Charles Rennie Mackintosh and Frank Lloyd Wright. Christopher Hussey's *The Life of Sir Edwin Lutyens* (Country Life, London, 1950 – part of the *Lutyens Memorial* volumes) might be considered one of the finest architectural biographies in the English language. More recent and more revealing biographies have been provided by his daughter and great-granddaughter: Mary Lutyens, *Edwin Lutyens by His Daughter* (John Murray, London, 1980), and Jane Ridley, *The Architect and his Wife* (Chatto & Windus, London, 2002). The best of the architect's correspondence with his wife is published in Clayre Percy and Jane Ridley, eds., *The Letters of Edwin Lutyens* (Collins, London, 1985).

A few books on the architect and his work can be particularly recommended: Roderick Gradidge, *Edwin Lutyens: Architect Laureate* (George Allen & Unwin, London, 1981); Margaret Richardson, *Sketches by Edwin Lutyens* (Academy Editions, London, 1994); Jane Brown, *Lutyens and the Edwardians: An English Architect and His Clients* (Viking, London, 1996); and then there are the several essays in *Lutyens: The Work of the English Architect Sir Edwin Lutyens (1869–1944)* (Arts Council of Great Britain, London, 1981), the book of the exhibition mounted in London in 1981–2, and those in Andrew Hopkins and Gavin Stamp, eds., *Lutyens Abroad* (British School at Rome, London, 2002). Lutyens's relationship with Gertrude Jekyll is discussed by Jane Brown in her *Gardens of a Golden Afternoon. The Story of a Partnership: Edwin Lutyens and Gertrude Jekyll* (Allen Lane, London, 1982) and *The Pursuit of Paradise: A Social History of Gardens and Gardening* (Harper Collins, London, 1999). A comprehensive bibliography, providing references to valuable writing on Lutyens by, amongst others, Robert Byron, H. S. Goodhart-Rendel, John Summerson and Lawrence Weaver, is in my own *Edwin Lutyens: Country Houses* (Aurum, London, 2001).

THE WAR GRAVES COMMISSION

The Unending Vigil: A History of the Commonwealth War Graves Commission 1917–1967 by Philip Longworth was the principal published source on Fabian Ware and his Commission, but now there is also David Crane's superb study and biography, *Empires of the Dead: How One Man's Vision Led to the Creation of WWI's War Graves* (William Collins, London, 2013). There is also Edwin Gibson and G. Kingsley Ward, *Courage Remembered: The Story behind the Construction and Maintenance of the Commonwealth's Military Cemeteries and Memorials of the Wars of 1914–1918 and 1939–1945* (HMSO, London, 1988). Fabian Ware gave his own account in *The Immortal Heritage* (Cambridge University Press, Cambridge, 1937). My own *Silent Cities* (London, 1977), which accompanied the exhibition of the memorial and cemetery architecture of the Great War held at the RIBA's Heinz Gallery, deals both with the prehistory and the architects of the Imperial War Graves Commission. *The Silent Cities* was also the title of the illustrated guide to the war cemeteries by Sidney C. Hurst (Methuen, London, 1929). Cemeteries of both world wars are illustrated in *Their Name Liveth* (Methuen, London, 1954) and in the annual reports of the Commonwealth War Graves Commission, while the foundation and work of the Commission is discussed in great detail in Mark Quinlan, *Remembrance* (Authors On Line, Hertford, 2005).

The architecture of the cemeteries in France by Lutyens is analysed by David Crellin in his article '"Some corner of a foreign field": Lutyens, Empire and the Sites of Remembrance' in Andrew Hopkins and Gavin Stamp, eds., *Lutyens Abroad* (British School at Rome, London, 2002), and by Sissi Castellano in 'Sir Edwin Lutyens e i cimiteri della Grande Guerra nel nord della Francia' in *Casabella* 675, February 2000 (Milan) and, more recently, by Tim Skelton & Gerald Gliddon in *Lutyens and the Great War* (Frances Lincoln, London, 2008) and by Jeroen Geurst, *Cemeteries of the Great War by Sir Edwin Lutyens* (010 Publishers, Rotterdam, 2010).

French, German and Italian war memorials and cemeteries are discussed in *A Celebration of Death* by James Stevens Curl, republished as *Death and Architecture* (Sutton, Stroud, 2002), and by Edwin Heathcote in his *Monument Builders: Modern Architecture and Death* (Academy Editions, Chichester, 1999). German war memorials are illustrated in Siegfried Scharfe, ed., *Deutschland über Alles: Ehrenmale des Weltkrieges* (K. R. Langewiesche, Leipzig, 1940), and the history of the German war graves organisation is given in *50 Jahre Dienst am Menschen, Dienst am Frieden* (Volksbund Deutsche Kriegsgräberfürsorge e.V., Kassel, 1969). The problems faced in creating war cemeteries and memorials are discussed in Rudy Koshar, *From Monument to Traces: Artefacts of German Memory 1870–1990* (University of California, Berkeley and Los Angeles, 2000), and Tischler's works are described in the essay by Meinhold Lurz in E. Mai and G. Schmirber, eds., *Denkmal-Zeichen-Monument* (Prestel, Munich, 1989) and by Gunnar Brands in his essay, 'From World War I Cemeteries to the Nazi "Fortresses of the Dead": Architecture, Heroic Landscape, and the Quest for National Identity in Germany' in Joachim Wolschke-Bulmahn, *Places of Commemoration: Search for Identity and Landscape Design* (Harvard University Press, 2001). For the Italian memorials, which deserve more attention, see Anna Maria Fiore, 'I sacrari italiani della Grande guerra' and other essays in Maria Giuffrè, Fabio Mangone, Sergio Pace & Ornella Selvafolta, eds, *L'architettura della memoria in Italia: Cimiteri, monumenti e città 1750–1939* (Skira, Milano, 2007). For the United States, see Elizabeth G. Grossman, 'Architecture for a Public Client: The Monuments and Chapels of the American Battle Monuments Commission' in the *Journal of the Society of Architectural Historians*, xliii, May 1984, and Dean W. Holt, *American Military Cemeteries* (Jefferson, NC, 1992).

MEMORIALS TO THE MISSING

The Memorials to the Missing, by Lutyens, Blomfield and others, are covered in the literature dealing with the work of the Imperial/Commonwealth War Graves Commission, cited above. The material in this chapter about the anxieties of the French about the number and scale of the memorials the British and other governments proposed to erect on their soil is derived from the files on St Quentin and Thiepval in the archives of the Commonwealth War Graves Commission.

THIEPVAL

Thiepval before and during the war is described in Lyn Macdonald's *Somme* (Michael Joseph, London, 1983), an excellent and impressive book both for its analysis of the campaign and for the testimonies of survivors. A detailed account of the military actions at Thiepval, the Schwaben Redoubt and the Leipzig Redoubt is given by Gerald Gliddon in *The Battle of the Somme: A Topographical History* (Alan Sutton, Stroud, 1994), originally published as *When the Barrage Lifts* in 1987 (Gliddon Books; Leo Cooper, London, 1990), and by Michael Stedman in his *Battleground Europe* guide *Somme: Thiepval* (Leo Cooper, London, 1995). John Masefield's book on *The Old Front Line, or the Beginning of the Battle of the Somme*, first published in 1917, has been republished with a preface by Martin Middlebrook and an introduction by Col. Howard Green (Pen and Sword, Barnsley, 2003).

The evolution of the design of the Memorial to the Missing of the Somme is discussed in some of the books on Lutyens listed above and is analysed in volume three of A. S. G. Butler, *The Architecture of Sir Edwin Lutyens* (Country Life, London, 1950), which formed part of *The Lutyens Memorial*. The best and most comprehensible discussion of the most complex form of the Thiepval arch is perhaps that by Roderick Gradidge in his essay 'Edwin Lutyens: The Last High Victorian' in Jane Fawcett, ed., *Seven Victorian Architects* (Thames & Hudson, London, 1976).

LEGACY

My account of the subsequent history of the Thiepval Memorial is largely derived from the files in the archives of the Commonwealth War Graves Commission. The opinions expressed about the significance of Thiepval are of course my own, but I am pleased to find how much they concur with those of Geoff Dyer in his remarkable, brilliant book *The Missing of the Somme* (Hamish Hamilton, London, 1994). Another recent and illuminating work which examines the wider implications of the dreadful legacy of violence and trauma created by the First World War is *1914–1918: Understanding the Great War* by Stéphane Auderin-Rouzeau and Annette Becker, two historians who were co-founders of the Historial de la Grand Guerre at Péronne (Profile, London, 2002).

For the posthumous reputation of the great architect of the Somme Memorial at Thiepval, see my article 'The Rise and Fall and Rise of Edwin Lutyens' in the *Architectural Review*, clxx, November 1981.

LIST OF ILLUSTRATIONS

*NOTE: Unless otherwise stated, the photographs were taken by
the author, mostly in 1990.*

ACKNOWLEDGEMENTS

I am most grateful to Mary Beard and to Peter Carson for seeing the point of my proposal to treat the Memorial to the Missing of the Somme as the equal of the Parthenon, the Alhambra and Westminster Abbey in the 'wonders of the world' series, and to Andrew Franklin for suggesting that this book be republished, with an afterword, a decade later. Thanks are especially due to John Harris, who asked me to organise the *Silent Cities* exhibition held at the RIBA Heinz Gallery in 1977 and in whose company I first visited Thiepval almost forty years ago. He was responsible for unifying my admiration for Lutyens's architecture with my long-standing obsession with the tragedy of the Great War, resulting in a conviction that the Thiepval Memorial is one of the most significant and telling monuments of the last century.

For their kind and generous help with the matter and text of this book, I must thank Rosemary Hill, Peter Howell, Martin Meade, Margaret Richardson and Jane Ridley, and I am particularly indebted to the staff at the Commonwealth War Graves Commission in Maidenhead – Maria Choules and Peter Francis – for assisting me in my research and cheerfully coping with my many questions. I should also like to thank John Garfield and Lyn Macdonald for their help with the illustrations.

INDEX

WONDERS OF THE WORLD

This is a small series of books that focus on some of the world's most famous sites or monuments. Their names are familiar to almost everyone: they have achieved iconic stature and are loaded with a fair amount of mythological baggage. These monuments have been the subject of many books over the centuries, but our aim, through the skill and stature of the writers, is to get something much more enlightening, stimulating, even controversial, than straightforward histories or guides. The series is under the general editorship of Mary Beard. Other titles in the series are: